Where Hope Blooms

The Widow's Path to Wholeness

Where Hope Blooms

The Widow's Path to Wholeness

Virginia L. Jelinek

CROSSLINK
PUBLISHING

Where Hope Blooms: The Widow's Path to Wholeness

℘ CrossLink Publishing / Castle Rock, CO

Copyright, © 2017 Virginia L. Jelinek

ISBN 978-1-63357-113-6

Library of Congress Control Number: 2017945007

Unless otherwise noted, all scripture quotations are taken from the New King James Version®. Copyright 1982 by Thomas Nelson, Inc. Used by permission. All rights reserved.

Scripture quotations marked "BBE" are taken from the Bible in Basic English (Public Domain).

Scripture quotations marked (CEB) are from the Common English Bible®, CEB® Copyright © 2010, 2011 by Common English Bible.™ Used by permission. All rights reserved worldwide. The "CEB" and "Common English Bible" trademarks are registered in the United States Patent and Trademark Office by Common English Bible. Use of either trademark requires the permission of Common English Bible.

Scripture quotations marked "MSG" are taken from The Message. Copyright © 1993, 1994, 1996, 2000, 2001, 2002. Used by permission of NavPress Publishing Group.

Scripture quotations marked "NIV" are taken from THE HOLY BIBLE, NEW INTERNATIONAL VERSION®, NIV® Copyright © 1973, 1978, 1984, 2011 by Biblica, Inc.™ Used by permission. All rights reserved worldwide.

Where Hope Blooms explores the faith-shaking experiences of widowhood. A deeply personal and richly emotive book, author Virginia Jelinek employs biblical stories and texts to illustrate the experience of bereavement common to those who are widowed. She understands the dark silence of grief and the lingering pain of loss from the inside of her own soul. She lights a candle in that darkness to illuminate a path back to faith and wholeness. I am deeply moved by this much-needed book.
-**Rev. Dr. Robert Cook,** Pastor of Christ United Methodist Church, Waynesboro, PA

Written from a heart that understands, *Where Hope Blooms* offers comfort and that elusive thing called hope to all those who've experienced the loss of their husbands. Beautifully written and full of godly insights, this book is one to savor. Highly recommended.
-**Gayle Roper,** *A Widow's Journey*

Virginia's book is about discovery, living in God's grace, allowing grief to do its healing, and yielding way to the birth of something new. As a pastor, my head is brimming with ideas of how to use this in the congregation, with widows, yet also with anyone who takes their spiritual life seriously, for she carves out a path toward spiritual wholeness for us all.
-**Barbara Hutchinson,** Episcopal Priest, Rector of St. Andrew's Episcopal Church, Shippensburg, PA

In *When Hope Blooms*, Virginia unmasks the pain of widows who often suffer in silence and reveals God's healing truth—you are not alone! If you're a widow stuck in your brokenness, fearing others will judge the depth of your grief, this Bible study is for you.
-**Pat Verbal,** Sr. Manager of Publishing & Ministry Resources at Joni and Friends' Christian Institute on Disability. Author, and

managing editor/contributor of the Beyond Suffering Bible (Tyndale Publishers 2016)

The loss of someone we deeply love takes us on a journey of widowhood that is different from any other journey we've experienced, and takes us to a different place in our relationship with God. As a widow, this book takes me to the One who has the Words of Life. A wonderful resource for The Body of Christ!
-**Janet Johnson**, Bible Study teacher, Counselor, Founder/Director of House of Grace women's ministry, Chambersburg, PA

Like the woman who wrote Song of Songs, Virginia knows from personal experience that love is strong as death and passion is fierce as the grave. Thankfully she has the grace to take us all with her on God's healing journey.
-**Frank Ramirez**, Senior Pastor of Union Center Church of the Brethren, Nappanee IN

Virginia Jelinek has a heart for widows. Her book, *Where Hope Blooms*, shares the richness of her experience of being a widow. Virginia writes wisely and well from the depths of her journey. The questions she wrestles with and the queries she poses engage the reader in her own seasons of loss and grief. There is a lot of wisdom in these pages for any who seek to enter their loss with an attentiveness to self and a heart for God's invitation amidst all that aches and hurts. The book is structured with reflections and chapter exercises that work for both individual exploration and group engagement. I recommend it to all who are experiencing loss and especially to those who have been ushered into widowhood
-**Glenn Mitchell,** Director of Oasis Ministries in Camp Hill, PA

"Now she who is really a widow, and left alone, trusts in God and continues in supplications and prayers night and day."

1 Timothy 5:5

Contents

Acknowledgements

My deepest appreciation to those who helped this book evolve:

To my pastor, The Reverend Barbara Hutchinson; I thank her for encouraging me to embrace the authoring of this book as a God-given assignment, a suggestion that inspired me with vision and the spiritual energy with which to take-on and accomplish the task.

To Pam Williams, author of several books, editor, blogger, and dear friend whose gift of encouragement, patience, and editorial insights consistently offered me direction throughout the course of writing this book. I owe her much. Years ago, at the beginning of my writing career, she became my writing mentor. Her support, knowledge, and encouragement helped me to find, as a writer "my voice," without which this book would have been impossible to write.

To Cindy Karns, a precious friend and an avid reader with keen eyes who worked as an editorial assistant, spending countless hours searching for oversights on the manuscript and confirming its Scripture references. Thanks to her husband, Pat, for the times he worked alongside her. I could not have completed this book without their dedicated assistance and encouragement.

To Brianna Renshaw, editor, writer, and a friend for whom I owe much for her work in editing an earlier version of the manuscript. Her insightful wisdom gave me solid direction, confirming the theme of hope as the book's core message.

To Cheryl Andreus, close friend and confidant, a widow with whom I have much in common. Her prayerful support and perspective on widowhood played an important part in this book's formation and writing.

To Paula Kneer and Jan Rose, widows who graciously read parts of early versions of the manuscript. Bless you for giving me your insightful feedback.

To my four daughters whose love, support, and suggestions have meant much to me. Thanks to all my wonderful eleven grandchildren who breathe continuous joy into my life. Special thanks to granddaughters, Hannah, Torri, and Laura, each assisting me in some way, helping to bring my vision for this book to life.

To my extended family that graciously supported me throughout the book's writing; Tim and Sheila Ford, Donna Everritt, and Fran McCrobie, thank you for your valuable input, listening ears, and prayers.

To three widows in particular, Pat Grim, Ruby Beidel, and Florence Clawson, I express grateful appreciation. These women faithfully encircled me with their prayers and became members of a team of widows who read portions of this manuscript, looking up the Scriptures, and answering the questions. Their enthusiastic response to the readings and study portions confirmed the idea of using this book as a Bible study for widows.

To the many widows who have talked to me of their pain, and of their hopes, I express gratitude. I am especially appreciative of those who gave me permission to share pieces of their stories.

Lastly, I express appreciation to the many friends and others who throughout this book's writing have said to me sincerely, "I will pray for you." Every prayer prayed, I know, infused me with grace and strength.

I am forever grateful for all of the above peoples, each touching my life, directly or indirectly, helping me to accomplish what God had written on my heart to do.

Preface

Where Hope Blooms is designed to give you multiple ways to embrace and apply the information shared. One choice is to gain insights by reading only the narrative sections. However, if you desire an interactive reading experience, you can, in addition to reading the narrative, choose one or more of the exercises provided at the end of each chapter and work through them. The advantage of this method is that it permits you to go deeper into reflection, giving you opportunity to apply the truths you glean.

Another way you can use this book is as a small group study for widows. The purpose of such a study is two-fold. First, it offers a widow space in an environment where she can feel safe to talk, to cry and to receive ministry when needed. Secondly, it provides opportunity through doing the exercises with others to garner insights and perspectives you may not have considered on your own, encouraging and equipping you to face the many challenges of widowhood..

Participating in a group study involves the homework of reading the assigned chapters prior to the gathering. During the meetings, the facilitator will briefly summarize each chapter and guide the group through at least one exercise per chapter, more if time allows.

***

Suggested timeline for an eight-week group study

Week One: Chapters 1-3. Plan to do at least one exercise from each chapter. Repeat this pattern throughout the remaining weeks.

Week Two: Chapters 4-6

Week Three: Chapters 7-8

Week Four: Chapters 9-11

Week Five: Chapters 12-14

Week Six: Chapters 15-16

Week Seven: Chapters 17-18

Week Eight: Chapters 19

Introduction

All of us have a story to tell. Much of my story comes out of my personal experience with losing two husbands and the insights I have gained from my years as a widow. That said, I quote from *The Cloud of Unknowing,* "In the interior life we must never take our experiences as the norm for everyone else." I pray that through this book, the Scriptures it presents, and the questions it asks, that you will come to value your own story as the rich, unique, new beginning that God is inviting *you* to experience.

I look back on my first loss, a tragic moment in time when an auto accident suddenly whisked away from me John, my high-school sweetheart and husband of thirty-six years. I despised the grief that descended on me, stealing my cache of hope. My reaction was to run from the grief, an action that hindered me from healing and kept me searching for something or someone to ease my agony. Ultimately, that search led me into a second marriage. It was a foolish mistake. The union did not give me comfort—only additional pain and grief, resulting in a divorce.

In time, I met my third husband, William. After being married for seven years, he grew ill with cancer; his death terminated our sweet union and made me a widow once again. However, this time, not wanting to repeat my former history with grief, I chose to accept it, to honor it as God's means of healing, to see it as a teacher, one whose lessons would and did bring me healing and wholeness.

All of us approach our grief and widowhood differently, so your story may have little resemblance to my own. However, there is a commonality that joins widows, in the heartache we feel, in the struggles we have. Therefore, it is probable that as you read this book, you will see pieces of your own journey, places where you have found peace, but also areas where you may still feel stuck, unmotivated, unable to move on. Maybe you're a widow who finds herself dearly missing your spouse. You're weary of carrying a broken heart whose every beat makes you acutely aware of your loss. Perhaps you're a widow not knowing who you are anymore, wondering what your purpose is now. Then again, like many widows, you may feel the strain of a new-normal that has left you with responsibilities too heavy for you to carry alone.

Your face and the faces of our "sister widows" are the ones I've seen as I wrote this book. I am one of you. I know how you feel. The widowed life is not easy. The purpose in in my writing *Where Hope Blooms* is to give assurance, to let you know that wherever you are today in your widowhood journey, no matter how gloomy your life and future appear at present, the treasure of a rewarding and blessed life is your heritage; your loss cannot take that from you!

You might ask, "How can I find such treasure?

Reading this book will invite you to reset your focus. Then, much to your surprise, you'll find yourself, instead of counting all that loss has taken from you, asking, "Wait...what might I gain from this, from my pain—from my loss?"

It's a question that causes hope to bloom. We might consider it a "God invitation," asking us to embrace our widowhood. In doing so, we discover beauty hidden in the ashes of our loss, and also great treasure. We begin to see God in a new light, as our loving companion, ever beside us, leading us on the path with God-designed days, laced with blessings—a new beginning.

There is much Mystery in the spiritual life, offering us unlimited God invitations to explore, leading us into *ever-deeper* enrichment of soul. Widowhood—itself filled with mystery and so much unknowing—is an opportune time to accept God's invites, such as those addressed in this book.

Each God invitation we accept leads us to embrace the most important of divine mysteries, that which the Apostle Paul speaks of, "This mystery has been kept in the dark for a long time, but now it's out in the open. God wanted everyone...to know this rich and glorious secret inside and out, regardless of their background, regardless of their religious standing. The mystery in a nutshell is just this: Christ is in you..." (Colossians 1:26 MSG)

Christ in us—God in us. Dare a widow believe that this dynamic Life Source dwelling within her will allow her to experience peace that passes understanding, to trade despair for joy and to know hope that is always in bloom? I invite you to use this book to explore and discover the answer for yourself.

Finding Blossoms of Hope

"The dessert shall rejoice and blossom as the rose."

Isaiah 35:1b

CHAPTER 1

Longing for a Taste of Hope

"The waters have come up to my neck, I sink..."

Psalm 69:1b

I sat down in the doctor's office to fill out the new-patient form. I quickly penned in my name but stopped abruptly at the next line. Listed were four stations-of-life. Was I Married...Single...Divorced...Widowed?

My pen waited. I deliberated. Which am I?

Our life's station definitely sprinkles life with a particular flavor, doesn't it? The pleasant taste of my life had changed suddenly—drastically. A week prior the awful automobile accident had happened, taking the life of my husband of thirty-six years. Now here I sat, at the doctor's office for follow-up treatment of the injuries I suffered in that fatal event. My hopes dashed, life had lost its sweetness. Grief's bitter taste made sure of that.

I restudied the choices on the form. The silver band on my ring finger indicated married, but I wasn't; nor was I divorced—and certainly, I didn't consider myself single.

Pick one already—my mind commanded. The WIDOW option shouted loud demanding I claim my place at its table, to feed on its menu of sorrow. I despised the mandatory diet it presented, yet what choice did I really have? The title awaited my check-mark, the inking-in of my official "acceptance" of its unsavory role.

My acceptance that day of widowhood was not a placid, peaceful, "It is what it is," like my widow friend Cheryl frequently expresses. My acquiescence was nothing but a forced resignation to my new lot-in-life. Resentfully, my pen marked the W word, my defiance as pronounced as the little boy's, who when his mother instructed him to sit down immediately, said, "Okay, I'm sitting down on the outside—but—inside I'm still standing up!"

Inspirational author, Marilyn Beattie, often writes about the rewards of learning to accept our life's circumstances. She says, "Acceptance is the place from which all growth and change occurs."[1] Undeniably, change (unwilled and unwanted) had occurred in my life redefining me and my existence, transforming me into a widow, a self and skin I did not want to own or grow into—only shed.

At that stage, I could see no hope in widowhood—only a bleak life ahead filled with sadness and despair. My grief muddled thinking introduced the mistaken notion that hope would forever remain lost to me, until I had wiped clean from my plate all residue of sorrow. Naturally, escaping from grief's clutches as quickly as possible became my obsession.

As a novice to widowhood, I wanted to understand grief, this strange and unwelcome enemy who had invaded my life. I busied myself researching the then-limited resources on grief, desiring to unmask its agenda and find a way to outwit it. Much to my dismay, I discovered no plan, no escape route. I was stuck—up to my neck in it—whether I liked it or not.

One day though, recalling someone who had suffered loss saying that grief diminishes with time, a glimmer of hope grew in my mind. *Maybe if I attempt to daily measure grief by charting how I feel each new day, I will discover the weight of my grief is lessening—that it's actually shrinking each day!*

However, my scale of "how-do-I-feel-today?" consistently confirmed what I didn't want to own. The weight of my grief was rapidly growing, like an expanding sinkhole, an abyss determined to eat me alive. I panicked.

Hope—how quickly it dissolves in the presence of grief. Hope gone, fear whispered continually, "You'll never come out of this dark hole."

Inconsolable day and night, I longed for at least a crumb of hope and encouragement—something, anything—that promised quick deliverance from sorrow. I prayed constantly. Admittedly, my panic-filled pleas sounded less like prayer, more akin to a pathetic mantra. God, please remove this unbearable grief... God, please take away my sorrow... God, please...

Writer and playwright George Bernard Shaw is credited to have once said, "Most people do not pray, they only beg." His words describe perfectly my supplications back then in my seeking release from grief's grip. Yet, who in the throes of sorrow, seeing no hope on the horizon, doesn't beg for relief?

For several years after John's passing, begging prayers were my norm. Day after day, my prayers stuffed, not with faith-that-believes, but with shreds of unbelief and scraps of demanding pleas, would fly heavenward. Grief remained present, hope remained absent, making me think that the heavens had slammed shut and that the Sovereign's ears were deaf to my cries.

However, eventually I would come to understand that the Divine hears and answers begging prayers as well as faith-filled prayers. The latter is the express route, while begging pleas drag us, kicking and screaming, to God's throne. There we crash, exhausted, surrendering, depositing our baggage of demands and despair at the feet of the Divine. It's in that act of relinquishment that acceptance is born—and ultimately, hope springs, once more sweetening our life.

Exploration and sharing

Whether you're a new widow or one who's long traveled on its road, whether you deem yourself in a good place or in a not so good place in your widow's journey, take a few moments to ponder the exercises below. There are no right or wrong answers to the questions in this book—your replies are simply a part of your story of finding hope, healing, and wholeness.

Exercise 1:1

Recognizing that the way we perceive widowhood definitely affects our hope, use this exercise as a means of discovery. How do you presently perceive widowhood? Check below the ones that best describes your current perception. I see widowhood as:

- *A bane, a life full of hardship and trials.*
- *A dead end.*
- *A lot in life I did not ask for—one I can't do much about—just live it out.*
- *An opportunity to find promise hidden in its days, enriching me with personal and spiritual growth, affording me opportunities to help others who grieve.*

Exercise 1:2

Take a moment to reflect. Write out your response to the question below.

- How do you wish you could perceive your widowhood?

Exercise 1:3

Record your answers or if in a group, share your responses with others.

- Where do you see yourself presently on your grief's journey?
- What events or things have helped to bring you to the point of acceptance? Or, if you're not there yet, knowing it takes time, what progress are you seeing/making?
- In your widowhood, what have you considered positive milestones along your path? How so?
- How has your view of widowhood changed with the passing of time?

***

In his book, Out of Solitude, Henri Nouwen tells of a man diagnosed with cancer. Angry over his fate, he begged heaven for answers. "Why did this happen to me? What did I do wrong to deserve this fate?" Eventually, the man turned a corner, finding hope when he dropped that question and asked another—"What is the promise hidden in this event?"[2]

Using personal stories from my journey of losing two husbands—John in 1999, dying suddenly in an automobile accident, and William in 2012 from cancer, throughout this book I invite widows to explore with me similar questions, such as: What is the promise hidden in our widowhood? Where in the ashes of our loss will we find the "beauty" that Isaiah 61:2 advertises? How can we find hope in the darkness of our loss—in the many struggles of widowhood?

As we use this book to aid our exploration, whether we do it on our own or with a group, my prayer is that every reader will find hope and a genuine, warm sense of God's love and favor enveloping them.

Prayer suggestions

Quietly share with God any despair, loneliness, or angst you feel regarding your life as a widow. Pray for a taste of fresh hope. Pray for holy grace to accept widowhood. Ask for eyes of faith that see within the ashes of widowhood lie treasures of blessings. Pray for courage and endurance to obtain those riches. Pray for opportunities to help other widows

CHAPTER 2

Finding Hope in a Muddle of Mistakes

"When he came to his senses, he said ...I will...go back to my father..."

(Luke 15:17a-18a NIV)

After John died, my grief still raw, I daily questioned, "How long will I feel like this—encumbered with unbearable sorrow, dead inside?"

My young-adult children suggested, "Mom, just take one-day-at-a-time." However, that was an unrealistic goal; I barely could do a minute-at-a-time!

Grief, screaming within me, seemed relentlessly bent on destroying me. I had to master it if I hoped to survive. My goal-oriented-self rose to the challenge. "Mind-over-matter," I vowed. *"I will* overcome this grief; *I will* deal with it and get over it quickly. Grief will not rule me—or my life!"

Some of that resolve was a result of considering my loss of John as a test of my character, a pass or fail examination where

I had to prove to others my strength and spirituality. Certainly, those whom I had mentored in the past were watching to see my final grade, right? For them, and for my family, I feigned strength and faith, an illusion I began to believe.

My ignorant self-sufficient belief, *I am in charge—in control,* coupled with my lack of knowledge on how to cope with grief, had me packing up my sorrow (or so I thought) in record time, securing it in the closet of my heart, padlocking its door. I took to scripting out my days, scribbling plans across my once-full, now-empty pages of life; I impulsively wrote into place whatever promised the slightest chance of subduing sorrow and restraining grief. A mission—to reinvent my life as quickly as I could—took over, consuming me.

Driven by it, denying grief any voice, I plunged into one project after another. I had a new house built so I could leave the old memory-filled one behind. I opened the doors of my new home, starting a ministry to help hurting women. When that didn't seem enough to keep loneliness at bay, I searched for a new relationship and found one. My children saw it as unhealthy. I saw it with love hungry eyes. Temptation awakened, enticing me with options I conceded to. I proceeded, marrying the man.

I did all those things, of course, wearing a disguise—a mask of deception fooling outsiders—and myself. They, amazed at my "progress" remarked, "You've done so well in getting over your grief!" I agreed, fully convinced I had survived. I was over my loss—a delusion that soon proved disastrous.

Three years passed, each a year of agony. Throughout those years, I sorrowfully watched the life I had sought so hard to reconstruct fall apart. Relationships with my children crumbled. My second marriage—painful from the start—split. Weary, confused, emotionally beaten, full of shame and guilt, every ounce of self-sufficiency washed out of me, I surrendered. I had no will left to fight.

Author and speaker, Joan Chittister writes, "Loss and loneliness, darkness and depression all sear the soul and cleanse it from its sense of self-sufficiency."[1]

That was me; self-sufficiency erased, soul-seared, and soul-starved. My upcoming divorce proved the final straw. Everything I had hoped would eradicate grief from my life, like dandelion spores, had taken to the wind, vanishing. I was left empty—except for the stock pile of grief within that I had ignored for four-and-a-half years—untouched since John's death.

It rose within me like an unexpected tsunami, tossing me, filling me with terrible dread and fear. Feeling utterly forsaken with no one to blame but myself, I wondered, *what was I to do—where could I go?* I had lost my family's respect. They did not like the "reinvented" me I had created, nor want her around. I couldn't fault them; I didn't like her either—the stranger that lived inside me.

Overwhelmed with sorrow, I arrived at my life's lowest point. I had spent the years since John's death pursuing tangible things I had hoped would numb grief. Unfortunately, in trying to rid myself of it, I inadvertently had closed the door of my heart, turning the ears of my spirit nearly deaf to the Sacred. How could I now, seeing my embarrassing muddle of mistakes—the temptations I had heeded, the fiasco I had created—call on God for help?

I was convinced God viewed me as I saw myself; one big disappointment, a widowed-woman sinking in the quicksand of her mistakes.

Nevertheless, in the midst of that terrible time, I heard the Voice of grace and mercy sigh, as if tremendously relieved, "Finally—are you ready *now*—to allow grief to do its healing mission?"

I said yes.

For the first time in years, I tasted hope.

Explore and share

Mistake making and times of temptation are normal; they are a part of being human. Unfortunately, though, there's a greater chance of our flirting with temptation's suggestions in our lowest times—when hope seems remote; when we are missing our soul mate and the intimacies of married love, when hardship, unbearable stress, grief, and sorrow are present.

Exercise 2:1

Of today's society, Joan Chittister notes, "Guilt has gone out of fashion in the Western world."[2]
- How might today's air of permissiveness in our society influence the way we respond to temptation?

Exercise 2:2

Consider some biblical characters that battled temptation. Did they win or lose the battle?
- Sampson (Judges 16:5-6, 16-17)
- Joseph (Genesis 39:7-9)
- King David (2 Samuel 11:1-5)
- Regarding your personal widowhood experience thus far, has temptation been a battle at times—or no battle whatsoever? What factors explain your response?

Exercise 2:3

Ponder the following questions. If in a group setting, discuss your responses.
- How can we know when we are using rationalization or compromise to justify an act that will lead us astray?

- How important is it for us to be aware of our weak areas? Why?
- In what ways, might a widows' study/companion group serve to help one another in dealing with temptation?

Exercise 2:4

Read I Corinthians 10:13

- What direction and hope does this verse give us in times of temptation?

***

What if we do cave into temptation? Afterward, what will we do? Will we choose to sit in our muddle, embarrassed and ashamed of ourselves and the mistakes made, feeling alienated from God? Or will we opt to—similar to the Prodigal coming to his senses saying, "I will return to my father and admit I sinned against him"—rise from our muck with a repentant heart and head homeward?

Repentance never fails to lead us home—to hope that has no end—to the Divine's loving embrace where God's huge Father-heart robes us in heaven's best and joyfully shouts, "My child who was dead, is alive!"

Then, most amazingly, God mysteriously takes our snarled mess of mistakes, weaves them into a divinely beautiful story of mercy and grace, love and redemption. It's a story we are meant to share, helping other prodigals find their way home to God's love.

Prayer suggestions

David wrote Psalm 51, a prayer of repentance, following Nathan's visit. Thoughtfully read through its verses. Select the words that speak to your heart. Echo them to God as your prayer.

CHAPTER 3

Doing the Task of Grieving: Releasing Hope

"I will take up...weeping and wailing..."

Jeremiah 9:10

No woman is ever fully ready for widowhood. Even those widows whose life experiences have left them widowed previously, if they are widowed again, their heart has to learn all over how to let go—how to survive. I experienced this when, thirteen years after John's death, I married William Jelinek. We were only married seven years before he grew ill, cancer taking his life within eight months. The question, will I survive the pain of "this" loss? once more found a home in my thoughts.

As if synchronized to her husband exhaling his last breath, the "will-I-survive" question immediately awakens in the widow's mind following his passing. There it swirls like a growing tornado, sucking up all other thoughts, leaving only those of sorrow behind. Devastated, the widow watches grief—a lifetime supply—unpack its luggage. It intends to stay. In the future, even if she should find a new love and decides to remarry, the widow will discover grief for her deceased spouse remains intact. Hidden beneath a blanket of sweet sorrow, it forever claims ground in the widow's heart.

As stated in the previous chapter, after John died my way of answering, *Will I survive grief?* was to escape or ignore grief's pain. However, in 2012, when William passed, although his death initiated a new siege of widowhood with grief claiming yet more space in my heart, I reacted differently.

This time around, having gained some sense, I knew better than to play loose with grief. To repeat my sad history with it would destroy me. I determined to find an effective approach to grieving.

Knowing from experience that initial grief shows no mercy, I braced myself. I stood firm, refusing to closet my sorrow. I conceded to it, fully understanding that grieving one's loss is a task one has to attend to, no excuses permitted. If I had learned anything from my first round of widowhood, it was this: to practice truancy with grief is folly—it only sets you back, delaying its end. It kidnaps hope and healing until you pay its ransom.

Undoubtedly, grieving is one of life's hardest tasks. It takes perseverance and patience. Certainly then, some expertise is useful in order to do its work successfully. With that mindset, in the aftermath of William's death, desiring to grieve in a healthy way, I did research on "doing grief" correctly.

Occasionally, in the process of my research, I would hear or run across a remark about "attending" one's grief. The idea flipped a switch inside my brain, giving me hope that I had discovered a way to grieve in a productive, healthy manner. After all, as a mother, I had spent most of my life attending to my children, nurturing them, making sure their needs were met. Certainly, I could choose to do the same with grief—to respect, foster, claim, and take genuine care of *it*.

Thereafter, when grief would rush in, overwhelming me, I would *attend*—be present— at its session, allowing my emotions free expression. This act of attending seemed to open within my soul a portal through which grief could flow out of me. Sometimes that flow began with my voicing or shouting out what I was feeling at that moment. Other times, when anger stirred my emotions, choking me with a resentment for which I had no words, I found release in shaking my fists or hitting them against the wall, acts uncommon for me, but at that time they helped to vent what simmered within me.

Often, I attended my grief by encouraging myself to weep intensely. Rather than cutting my tears short when I felt grief grip me, trying to take control, I would let go and sob...and sob, gut-wrenching groaning that bore resemblance to a mother birthing a child, straining with each contraction. The emotions passing through me were like that—genuine physical contractions, bending me over with pain, as if tearing from my inner core an infant-sized piece of the grief that lived within me, releasing it so I need not carry its burden any longer.

In his book, *Loving Grief*, Paul Bennett talks about the need of actively attending to grief. "It's amazing," he says, "how often I must remind myself to touch my grief, to give it some attention and some time to be felt."[1]

Of course, it is unhealthy to dwell on nothing but grief, making of widowhood a vocation. However, the opposite is also true. Paying small attention to grief, failing to take time to consciously "touch" it, works against us. It denies grief its voice, ultimately hindering and delaying the healing we desperately yearn for. Undoubtedly, such denial is especially destructive to hope. It keeps it hostage; out to sea and out of sight, like a hijacked ship carrying supplies we desperately need to stay alive.

Every one of us grieves differently. All of us have to find our individual method of grieving. Naturally, since grieving is painfully difficult, it's natural to want to put it off, to refuse to deal presently with the heaviness we feel, inwardly hoping it will go away like a passing tummy ache. Grief though is resilient. It does not go away on its own. It simply sits inside the soul restrained by our efforts to silence it, churning, stewing within us, thickening our sorrow until we finally acknowledge and respect it.

Explore and share

When that lump of grief in our gut seems unusually heavy, we can learn to respond to it positively. We might consider it a signal calling us to do some active grieving, dedicating current time and space to literally touch our grief, to feel it coursing through us— permitting it to flow unhindered. Surprisingly, we'll find such "attending" lightens our present heaviness significantly, liberating hope to once again spill its bounty into our soul.

Exercise 3:1

If attending our grief has such merit, why would any of us hold back from touching it? There are reasons, of course. Here's a few. Check off the ones that have stopped you, at times, from personally attending your own grief.

- Fear: *I'm afraid that touching my grief will overwhelm and depress me.*
- Flawed thinking: *I see grief as an enemy I must fight if I want to survive.*
- Pride: *People are watching me. I must prove myself a victor— and the appearance of my faith as stronger than my grief.*
- Society's influence: *After the funeral and a few days off from work, society demands that I "buck up," put a smile on my face and return to normal. My co-workers and even some family members make me feel I should be done grieving. So, I've conditioned myself not to cry or show physical expressions of my grief, in public—and even at home.*

Exercise 3:2

If we take time to reflect on God's Word, we find it confirms and gives legitimacy to the task of physically attending to our grief. We see this in looking at biblical accounts of individuals in the process of grieving.

In the verses below, consider the mourners involved. Explore how they "attend" their grief, giving physical expression to their heartache. End this exercise asking, *what do their actions say to me that will help me fully attend my own grief?*

- Genesis 23:2; 37:32-34
- 1 Samuel 1:10
- 1 Chronicles 7:22
- Jeremiah 9:10a
- Ezekiel 21:6

Exercise 3:3

Attending our grief well, involves both times of withdrawing from others and drawing comfort from others. Unfortunately, although an abundance of comforters may have showed up at her spouse's funeral, a widow oftentimes finds few remain afterward at her side. The void hurts. When she most needs the presence of caring friends, the widow feels forsaken.

The sad fact is, her friends and acquaintances are not unlike many others. Not knowing how to comfort, or what to say, people often distance themselves from the grieving. Where then can the widow find a source of outside comfort? She learns in time the ones who *best* understand how to comfort the grieving are those who have experienced loss themselves.

Consequently, the intention of this exercise is to give widows awareness of where they can find others, or groups, who like themselves, are acquainted firsthand with grief. Begin by spending some time researching your local area for grief support groups such as Grief Share. Part of their motto is "You don't have to go through the grieving process alone," words they live up to. This link can tell you where one is in your area: https://www. griefshare.org/. Also, consider hospitals and medical facilities. Many of those offer grief classes, helping the griever to understand the grieving process, receive comfort, and have opportunity to meet others walking the same path.

Maybe you're presently sensing a need for socialization, a hunger for friends who genuinely understand what you're going through. If so, look for widows' groups in your town. You might start your search by contacting churches. A growing number of them, recognizing the widow's unique social situation, have formed widows' groups, offering occasions to socialize and make new friends.

Additionally, there is an abundance of online blogs for widows, designed to encourage and connect the widow to an online community of widows. It's an active community, birthing many friendships between widows.

It is vital to a widow's healing to reach out to others in her sorrow. Possibly, especially if you're an introvert, you have found that difficult to do, but it is crucial. Why? Because—oftentimes—the best way to attend your grief, is to share it with others, and who can better understand your pain than another widow?

Prayer suggestions

Pray that you might remain faithful to the task of healthy grieving, finding hope and healing in attending your grief. Pray that you might locate groups where you can connect with other grievers, finding relationships where you find comfort and give comfort. Pray that in attending your grief, you will look for—and encounter the Divine—the God of all comfort.

CHAPTER 4

Seeking Hope When Faith Lies Shattered

"I have heard of You by the hearing of the ear, but now my eyes see You."

Job 42:5

"Mom, you're welcome to use my car," my daughter suggested. Away at college, she had no present need for it.

I looked out the window at her vehicle sitting in the driveway. Instantly, my stomach knotted. Three weeks before, our family car had sat parked beside it. Today though, the family car sat in a junkyard, a smashed heap of tangled metal, a ghastly testimony to the death of the car's driver, John, my husband.

Miraculously, I had survived the accident. Grief-stricken and still nursing the injuries I had sustained in the wreck, I hadn't bought another car. I was in no rush. I wanted to stay safe, closeted at home—forever. The mere thought of getting into an automobile ever again gave me great angst.

However, this particular day, I had no choice. Urgent matters demanded I accept my daughter's offer, slide behind the steering wheel of her vehicle, and head for town.

Arriving at the town's traffic circle, I stopped at the yield sign and waited for opportunity to enter into the busy flow of traffic. Glancing into the car's rearview mirror, I froze. I watched a fast-approaching tractor-trailer truck nearing the car's backside. I had a fleeting thought— *will the truck plow into me?* — right before I heard the gnawing crunch of metal meeting metal. Immediately the car catapulted forward, coming to a stop where fortunately, I could steer the injured car to the curb.

Unnerved, I got out of the car waiting to speak with the approaching truck driver. My thoughts racing, I tried to comprehend what had just transpired. *Why did God permit this to happen—another accident—while I am still raw from the one that took John's life three weeks ago?*

Fighting tears, the thought, *at least the accident wasn't my fault,* gave me relief, but that consolation vanished when the trucker drew near booming, "LADY, WHAT WERE YOU DOING?"

Astounded, I wasted no time. I hailed the police officer across the street. Unfortunately, he reported he had not witnessed the accident, but he agreed to record the details. I pointed to the yield sign to justify my actions. The trucker offered his side of the story, fabricating a lie, "Officer, she started forward and then suddenly stopped..."

The impatient police officer, obviously irritated, closed his notepad abruptly and walked off, leaving Trucker and me to our arguing. He, refusing to bend, and I, already involved in a war over my husband's life insurance policy, did not want another battle to fight. I conceded. Trucker walked away, his driving record un-marred. I would pay out-of-pocket to get my daughter's car fixed.

All the way home, I wept a redundant thought. Is this how the life of a widow goes—one trouble after another?

Job's words, "I expected good but evil showed up" (Job 30:26 MSG) perfectly expressed my sentiments that day.

That incident with the trucker, following so closely on the heels of the auto accident that took John's life, seemed a final straw, breaking me and shaking my faith, forever altering its landscape. The One I had called Friend and Savior, the God who through the years had faithfully proved trustworthy, the Divine Being that had always showed up in my hours of need, now appeared gone, leaving me to fate, my faith crushed.

I thought I knew God, but did I? Based on the ways that I had experienced the Divine in the past, God's "new" behavior appeared strange, unfamiliar, and uncharacteristic of The One called Love, who promises, "I will never leave you or forsake you" (Hebrews 13:5).

I secreted from others the God-doubts and questions simmering within me. I wasn't used to wearing the shoes of a skeptic. I felt guilty, a condemned heretic, for harboring thoughts contrary to what I had been taught. My religious upbringing had looked unfavorably on asking hard questions regarding the Divine—and yet—here I was angry with God, full of questions. Sadly, hope's voice grew silent within me, as often happens when guilt moves in, adding additional pain to one's suffering.

Preacher and theologian, Reverenced Peter Gomes wrote, "Suffering makes us ask hard questions of God... [such as] where were you when I needed you?" Gomes continued, "Suffering also makes us ask hard questions of ourselves... [such as] ...What have I done to deserve this?"[1]

Part of CS Lewis' suffering after his wife died of cancer, included a time of questioning his faith, and lashing out at God. He, a Christian apologist, writes of this experience in "A Grief Observed." He notes that grief acquaints us with the God that he (Lewis) called, the "great iconoclast," the "smasher of holy images."[2] He was referring to the personal beliefs we individually adopt as our God-conceptions-—the many God-photos we carry in our spiritual wallet that support our faith—only to discover through a faith-testing experience, our concepts of "who God is" are often riddled with false assumptions.

Explore and Share

Our personal God conceptions, accurate or faulty, give us expectations of how we believe God will (or should) perform in any given situation. There are plenty of examples in the Scriptures of people whose God-conceptions were shattered when misfortune came their way. The shattering though, unbeknownst to the participants, would prove a divine happening, an unveiling of God, leaving each awed, their faith enlarged, their hearts blessed with a greater understanding of the Divine.

Exercise 4:1

Read John 11:21, 32

In this exercise, we find close friends of Jesus, Mary and Martha, grieving the death of their brother.
- What were their expectations of Christ? Were they met?
- Do you think the sisters may have felt some anger toward Jesus for dashing their hopes?
- They both voice the same remark (v. 21, 32) when they see Him. How does the way they phrase their words, reveal an intentional message, showing their disappointment in His delayed arrival?
- How about each of us: like Mary and Martha, in what ways have you seen some of your hopes shattered?
- In times when you've felt disappointed in God's timing or movement in your life, did you hold it silently within, or like the sisters, openly express your feelings to God? How

can expressing to God—your disappointment in God—be helpful to your spiritual life?

Exercise 4:2

Read Mark 4:35-41

In this story, we find the disciples on a boat in a life-threatening storm, a faith-testing time when some of their God-expectations are lost at sea.
- What had led them to make the boat trip in the first place? (v. 35)
- As they left the shore, how might having Jesus on board lead them to believe they would have a pleasant, safe crossing to the other side?

Of course, in reading this story we find the crossing proved other than pleasant! Let's imagine for a moment the disciples, when, in the midst of dedicatedly following Christ, everything goes wrong.
- Thunder cracking, lightning flashing, drenching rain descends and gigantic waves rise, threatening to drown the boat—and Jesus is missing from the scene. What do you think the rain-soaked disciples, working feverishly to keep the craft afloat, might be thinking regarding the missing presence of Christ when He is most needed?
- When the disciples go looking for Jesus and find Him asleep, they awaken Him. What hard, doubt-filled question do they ask Him?
- Like the disciples setting out in their boat, fearless with Jesus in their midst, never expecting to encounter a horrific storm, how often is our faith based on perception—of what we think God will permit—or not permit to happen to us? How might we let our faith grow beyond our perceptions?

- Like the disciples, are we presently carrying any concerns that have us asking or thinking, "God, don't you care...?"

***

The good news regarding all of our God-doubts and questions is, as CS Lewis wrote in his faith-shattering season, "[This] shattering is one of the marks of [God's] presence."

In that light, we find assurance. In spite of our anger with the Divine, our God-doubts and questions, we can rest, they give—concrete evidence—of God at work in our lives. Therein, although we may feel distanced and far from God, the truth is, we are the opposite; we are residing in the Presence of God!

How can that be true? Because every faith-shaking experience, every hard question, every doubt, as the disciples discovered when they saw Jesus speak peace to the mighty winds, is actually an invitation—from God—to discover a fuller unveiling of "Who" God is.

Jesus encouraged asking questions, saying to us, "Ask, and it will be given to you; seek and you will find..." (Matthew 7:7). Accordingly, God inquiries and doubts dress us in the sackcloth of a humble pilgrim searching for truth.

Seeking truth and deeper understanding of God and God's ways is difficult work; it's soul-enlarging labor that often can only be done with a pickaxe—of questions—with which we crack the surface and go within ourselves. Slowly we dig our way through layers of faulty beliefs, until we finally come to the Bedrock of Truth, where gems of fresh understanding and revelation about ourselves and about God await us.

Best of all, through our questions—our digging, we find a new God-photo for our wallet: God—as Eternal Hope—the Restorer of faith in whose Presence "we live and move and have our being" (Acts 17:28). Our seeking has done its work. Along with Job we say to God, "I have heard of You by the hearing of the ear, but now my eyes see You" (Job 42:5).

___

Prayer suggestions

Pray for a seeker's heart. Pray for strength, for courage that will withstand faith shattering moments. Pray to honor, not despise, times of testing when God-questions surface...when you feel disappointed in the Divine's plan...when you think God does not care. Pray for open ears in life's storms, that in its winds you will hear God's invitation to know and experience God more fully.

CHAPTER 5

Hope: Out of Season

"Look at the birds of the air...Consider the lilies of the field."

Matthew 6:26a, 28b

Week after week following John's death in 1999, I would awaken to the same thought, "John is dead." Then the tears would start—again. One morning though, with the onset of tears, it seemed as if John himself walked into the room to give me a message. In my mind, I heard his voice clearly say, "Stop weeping. Celebrate life, not death."

I needed to hear those words. However, at the same time, I wondered, *how do I celebrate life in the midst of a tragic loss?*

A few months later, I received insight regarding that question. It happened when I was with my grandson, Jared.

Jared, out of all our then-six grandchildren, looked most like John (or "Pap-Pap" as the grandkids had called him). He had John's twinkling blue eyes and his grandfather's perceptivity, acute for a ten-year-old. It seemed ironic, totally unfair, and a cruel twist of fate that the car accident that took his Pap-Pap's life had happened on Jared's tenth birthday.

Following the accident, Jared never spoke of it or his grandfather. He went from being a happy child to an unusually quiet one, downcast even, with his head often bowed, as if a great weight rested on his shoulders. Sadly, his eyes no longer twinkled—evidence that the burden he shouldered had grown too heavy for his young soul to bear.

I wanted to hold him close, to tell him, "It's okay"—to speak something that might ease his pain, or help him to voice it—but it was *not* okay. When do loved ones *ever* consider the death of their family member acceptable?

Several months passed. Jared remained withdrawn. One day, he and his seven-year-old sister, Torri, accompanied me on some errands. The car's engine circulated toasty warmth on that cold day, yet Jared sat stiff in the back seat, his arms wrapped tightly around himself. He remained silent. His sister sat beside him, chattering happily.

Then, in an instant, without warning, the dam inside Jared broke. Sobbing profusely, he wailed, "Grammy, why did Pap-Pap have to die on my birthday? God must think I am a bad boy."

His words pierced my heart. What could I say, how could I speak peace to his troubled heart?

The words I spoke surprised me. I heard myself speaking wisdom, life-giving words, totally unlike the language of grief that had filled my mouth and thoughts over the past months.

"Jared, God knows you are a good boy," I began, not knowing quite where I was headed. "Pap-Pap's death is not punishment. Yes, the timing of his death is hard to understand. But Jared, look at it this way."

I continued, "Since it happened on your birthday, the day we celebrate YOU, then on October tenth of every year—the anniversary of Pap-Pap's death—we will always have something wonderful to celebrate—your birthday! It will help us celebrate life instead of thinking about death and being sad."

"Wow," said Torri, squeezing her brother's arm. She chirped sweetly, "Jared that makes you *special!*"

"Yeah," he said. "I never thought of it that way!"

I looked at Jared in the rear-view mirror. The luster had returned to his eyes—a sign of a heart set free of its load.

I've never forgotten that day's discussion. It helped Jared—and me, as well. It provided me a tiny taste of fresh hope, reminding me that even in the darkness of grief, there is always *something* to celebrate.

Explore and share

In our sojourning through widowhood, especially early on, hope can appear out of season. Its nectar lacking from our existence silences joy, giving our weary feet no reason to dance, our heart no cause to celebrate life.

Where can we possibly find blossoms of hope in grief's winter?

Hope, of course, can be found in something as simple as a song, a hug, a baby's giggle, or in a conversation chiming with refreshing insight, as happened to me that day with my grandson. Sometimes though, to bore a hole through our glacier of grief, something more pronounced is required, a resource guaranteed to bring us hope. There is such a supply; it's called creation, acclaimed and celebrated by its Creator as "good...very good" (Genesis 1).

We could say that God's creation is like a bank from which we can withdraw endless hope. Lady Bird Johnson, a nature lover, made consistent withdrawals from nature's vault, teaching her, "Where flowers bloom, so does hope."

Who wouldn't agree with her findings? Hope never fails to blossom in the hearts who take note of nature's offerings. For instance, when morning dawns, creation delights in surprising any observer. Our mouths drop, our eyes gape as we witness darkness surrendering to light, the sun rising as victor, as an elegant queen unfurling her glory, lavishly stretching her lacy fingers across the horizon painting it in exquisite colors.

Indeed, it seems God's creation is determined to lavish hope on us. Maybe nature does so by capturing our attention, opening our ears to hear an orchestra of birds ending their day in an evening song—or opening our eyes to the sight of snowflakes silently dressing the earth in a gown of white.

We never know when or where creation will stop us to show us something profound but this we know: even the simplest of creation's sightings can leave us awed, humbled, baptized with fresh hope—touched by God's presence.

Exercise 5:1

Read Matthew 6:25-31

In this Scripture, Jesus is speaking to a multitude, a crowd of ordinary people carrying life's burdens. Mourners, struggling with loss; parents, concerned about meeting the needs of their families; the homeless, wondering how much longer they can survive without food and shelter; the ill, looking for remedies—Jesus sees them all—hears every one of their silent cries. He speaks a message to them, His voice filled with compassion.

- What objects of nature does Jesus ask the people to look at and consider?
- How does Christ use these objects of nature to illustrate God's provision?
- What hope do you think the crowd heard in Christ's message that day?
- What hope do you hear in it for yourself?

Exercise 5:2

The book of Romans, speaking of creation says, "Open your eyes and there it is! By taking a long and thoughtful look at what God has created, people have always been able to see what their eyes as such can't see..." (Romans 1:19b-20a MSG).

- Describe a moment when nature—opened your spirit eyes and ears—to hear and see beyond the physical realm.
- What insight filled your heart in those moments? Did it give you hope?

It is a pure mystery how hope blooms when we pause to take "long and thoughtful" looks at nature's offerings. When we do, something amazing happens. Awareness comes, bringing to us a holy hush. It's then we realize the moment is sacred; we're standing on holy ground in communion with the Creator of the Universe. In a flash, our soul regains perspective. We know that life is much bigger than the sorrow we carry in our heart. It's a revelation that gives us cause for celebrating life!

***

Renowned author of *Pilgrim at Tinker Creek*, Annie Dillard, writes of her nature discoveries. "I stood alone, and the world swayed. I am a fugitive and a vagabond, a sojourner seeking signs."[1]

Widows are much the same; our world has swayed. We are alone, sojourners ever seeking signs of hope as we travel though widowhood. The good news is, we are certain to find it. We're sure to discover—that hope is always in season—to any heeding Christ's instructions, "Look at the birds...Consider the lilies."

Prayer suggestions

Pray to grow increasingly mindful of creation, to find time to walk in it and ponder its offerings. Thank and praise God for what you see and hear in nature's backyard. Pray for a discerning heart, ready to receive insights and lessons from your encounters with nature. If your location limits opportunities to view nature, thank God for photographers who bring nature to you through photobooks or websites such as http://www.naturespicsonline. com/. Thank God for the hope nature speaks to your heart.

CHAPTER 6

Taking Flight on the Wings of Hope

"Where then is my hope? As for my hope, who can see it?"

Job 17:15

The new widow, despair in her eyes and tears in her voice, asks me the question every widow asks herself, "When will things get better? When will grief disappear?"

I hesitate to reply. I know what she hopes to hear but I must speak truth. I share with her what I have learned in my journey of losing two spouses. "Things will get better with time. Grief will definitely lessen, but it will never totally disappear."

I read the shock and disappointment on her face. *Grief—it won't leave for good? Where then is hope found?*

This chapter attempts to draw a rough outline of how the grieving process moves along and how that process affects one's hope. Why is it important to consider this? Largely because grief affects our minds.

At the onset of grief, doubts can overwhelm a widow to the point that at times, she may even question her sanity. Of course, there's no hope in that! Oftentimes, it's not until she's with other widows and in hearing them voice the exact things she is questioning and experiencing, that she realizes and admits, *I've thought something was wrong with my mind—but now I see, every widow has these thoughts and feelings!*

Before we go on to look closer at this issue of how grief affects the mind and, consequently, overshadow hope, let's remember that a widow's grieving knows no clear-cut path. Accordingly, the outline I present here is merely a general idea of what you may or may not experience.

Regarding the initial months of grieving, all of us know, they pass slowly, each seems an eternity. During that stage, it almost seems that hope and grief are in a contest, with grief conquering most days. When hope manages to siege a portion of a day, grief quickly counters, plays its hand, stealing the win—prevailing again. So, the match goes on, hope squelching grief, grief burying hope.

Time, of course, is a great healer, so gradually the widow finds herself coming into a new "stage." In this place on widowhood's turf, grief appears less cruel of an opponent, actually gifting the widow with temporary passes at times, permitting her an occasional good day here and there. On these blessed events, the widow dances in hopes embrace—but then—grief returns, taking back its waiver. Her dance partner loses once again.

Then, as more time passes, the widow comes to a milestone. At this stage of her journey, the widow takes heart. She says of grief, "I have *more* good days than bad ones," excellent days where hope prevails.

Finally, the widow arrives at a monumental point. Here she sighs with joyous relief. "It's *only once in a while*, that I have a rough day." In this location hope lives as the final victor, confirming, "Hope does not disappoint..." (Romans 5:5).

Wouldn't it be wonderful, if at that point, widows would no longer feel their sorrow? However, time and experience teach the widow that's not feasible. Her loss has left her wearing a permanent hole in her heart. Naturally then, she will always grieve her loss to some extent.

I attest to that fact. In the eighteen years since John's death and the five years since William's, I have come to terms with it. I am—and will be—for the rest of my life, a mourner. Lest I think otherwise, it takes but a memory of one of my spouses to confirm the real truth.

You know how it goes when memories stir the heart. A romantic song playing on the radio, the one you and your beloved called "our song"... an aroma of a food the two of you loved cooking and eating together... the sighting of someone who wears a likeness to your departed... the list goes on, triggers that set off a fresh volley of grief.

Each triggering costs you something—a painful twinge, a deep longing stirring within for the one who has passed. Tears beg to go free; you restrain them—lest they betray you and tell the world that loss has maimed you, left you with a broken heart.

Whether our loss came years ago, or just yesterday, it's wise to acknowledge that the love we carry in our heart's pocket for our departed spouse will never go away. Wisdom tells us to expect, throughout our widowhood, the possibility of random grief storms to pass our way, sudden squalls, soaking our soul with yesterday's sorrow.

Each grief storm, depending on its severity, has potential of leaving us sad, and like Job, lamenting, "As for my hope, who can see?" The forecast for our future, as seen in the aftermath of a harsh grief storm, can appear gloomier than hopeful. Accordingly, our thinking can go amuck, setting off a redundant dialogue of depressing thoughts common to widowhood's sojourners. *I'll never survive widowhood...I hate being a widow! The responsibilities loss has placed on my shoulders isn't fair...I am tired of its endless days where purpose seems a mystery, of nights of going to bed alone and lonely...I'm weary of seeing couples enjoying life together—it makes me envious. Why do they still have their spouse, but mine was taken?*

There's no sense in feeling guilty for having such oppressive thoughts. They come, as do grief storms, bundled as part of the package called "Widowhood."

However, we can begin to help ourselves when we live with the awareness that negative thinking is dangerous, it sabotages the widow. To allow even just one unhealthy thought to run rampant, is to open a floodgate of depressing thoughts, giving grief space—another win, and hope—to take yet another loss.

Explore and share

Exercise 6:1

Read 2 Corinthians 10:4-5

- How does this Scripture passage apply to negative thinking?
- When it comes to keeping hope winning in your life, what current thoughts do you need to demolish, or take captive?

Exercise 6:2

- According to Philippians 4:8, what types of thoughts embody wise and healthy thinking?

Exercise 6:3

Read Psalm 27:13; Philippians 4:6-7

Using the "clues" found in these verses, how might you train yourself to respond to unexpected grief storms and the stresses of life in a healthy way? Write your answers below.

- Psalm 27:13
- Philippians 4:6-7

***

Poet Emily Dickinson said, "Hope is the thing with feathers—that perches in the soul."[1] Taking her bird analogy and applying it to our widowhood gives us insight for what we can do in times when our thoughts turn negative. By capturing each unhealthy thought as it comes to us, replacing it with a healthy thought, we literally free hope from its perch.

Hope, beautiful hope—it's on her wings that we can rise from sorrow, and soar above grief's gray clouds.

Missionary Amy Carmichael wrote, "All weathers nourish souls."[2] That means, our future is as bright as God's promises—our storms of grief, evermore assuaged by hope.

Prayer suggestions

Pray for diligence in guarding your soul life. Pray to stay alert and conscious of your thoughts, screening them for any thought that will prohibit hope. Pray for eyes that will always see hope—even in the midst of a grief storm.

Tilling Transformation

"Fix your attention on God. You'll be changed from the inside out."

(Romans 12:2b MSG)

CHAPTER 7

Passing through the Desert of Dry Bones

"Our bones are dry, our hope is lost, and we ourselves are cut off!"

Ezekiel 37:11

Figuratively, the loss of a loved can throw us into a desert. It's a soul-parching place where we share the lament of those in today's Scripture. "Our bones are dry," bones from which the meat of our identity—the who we were prior to our loss—has been stripped clean, leaving us a skeleton of our former self.

In widowhood's desert land, our eyes are inclined to stay reverted on the past. We find no comfort in this wasteland. Our grief cries, seeking justice, wanting to make some sense of our senseless loss. Our minds pose questions. We tear them apart looking for answers—finding none, our despair only doubles.

The questions, day and night, fly like sparks into the air. One widow wails, *he was such a good man, why did he have to die? It makes no sense.* Another argues with the "unfairness" of death's timing, *we had so much to look forward to, why did he have to die now?* Other widows sob thinking, *why have my children been left without a father, a man who will never see them graduate, attend their weddings, or know the joy of grandchildren? Why was my husband chosen to die, leaving me alone; it's not fair!*

As if the questions are not enough, in the desert heat, anger scorches the mind. We may fume at doctors we believe failed to do enough...*my husband would be alive today if....* We may even rile against God's decree that all are appointed once to die (Hebrews 9:27), *why does life steal the treasures it gives?*

For sure, flocks of faith-eating vultures roam this desert's sky. Relentlessly, they attack, attempting to pick from our bones any remaining specks of hope, pieces of truth that we may be striving to hold onto—like the truth of God's promises in Jeremiah 29:11, "For I know the thoughts I think toward you...thoughts of peace and not of evil, to give you a future and a hope."

Every part of our widowhood journey has purpose. The significance of its desert is that it helps us work through our questions and anger, and teaches us the necessity of letting go of what we can't resolve. However, until we glean this understanding, we're prone to remain in it, using its space to yell at life for disillusioning and disappointing us, and to complain to God about singling us out, just as Job did. "What have I done to You...watcher of men? Why have You set me as Your target...?" (Job 7:20b).

Of course, this leaves our souls parched, completely unaware that our loss is not simply all about loss but—what we have yet to gain. Even if that awareness is present, we may not believe it as truth.

So, what is the reality here? Can our loss be transformed into what will actually profit us?

Ezekiel's story in chapter 37:1-14, would lead us to such a conclusion. It is an amazing story of loss followed by a radical transformation. His account begins as does our widowhood, in the desert with dried out bones, the evidence of lives once lived, once full of spirit, now spiritless.

In the story, God prods Ezekiel with a challenge, would you believe to prophesy to a desert full of brittle bones?! The prophet exercises his faith and shouts to his dead audience, "Let these bones live!"

Imagine, immediately the bones respond, clacking loudly, groaning, snapping into place. The skinless skeletons rise, standing tall on their bare-boned feet, and at Ezekiel's command, they grow instant skin. Nevertheless, they are still without spirit—remaining dead—only half-transformed, but then—the Breath of God blows over them. A miracle happens. Their spirits return. Resurrected from the dead, fully transfigured, life gets a second chance.

Priest Carrenda Baker often says, "God loves us too much to leave us where God finds us." That applies to the widowhood's desert where God's Spirit never tires of blowing sacred breath on dry bones crying out for spiritual transformation.

Such divine interventions though, usually require our cooperation. God can only do what we allow. As Ezekiel's vision points out, to make transformation a reality in our personal life, does require listening for, and responding to, God's prodding.

I recall my first time widowed. My inward disappointment with God's personalized plan for me, and my impatience with divine timing, closed my ears to holy nudges. Consequently, I lived in widowhood's desert an extraordinary long time.

However, when William passed things went differently. As I grieved his loss, angst grew, fearing I would return to widowhood's desert. As a prevention measure, I began diligently striving to keep my heart tethered, my hope resting on God alone. I started praying continuously to remain faithful and patient, but I was concerned: was prayer enough to keep me grounded? One day I heard God prodding, "Learn to see *Me* as your constant Companion, your Divine helper."

Putting God's nudge into practice took mindfulness, as it still does. By mindfulness, I mean a habit of keeping one's soul aware, and attentive to God's presence, remaining watchful and responsive to the Spirit's movement within the heart.

I remain amazed at the transformation that came as I attempted to heed God's request. Doing my best to consistently envision God as my Companion and Helper developed in me a steadfastness I had lacked. It deepened my love for the Divine, the holy Three-in-One, filling my spirit with a gentle, peaceful sense of God abiding within me, a Sacred Source from which I could draw strength, love, wisdom, and hope.

The transformation encouraged me to follow another of God's prompts. "Embrace your widowhood; make of it a spiritual pilgrimage, a quest to live in oneness with me." This made beautiful sense to me, ultimately filling fearful me with holy confidence when facing widowhood's hardships. What's more, it permitted me to view challenges as divine invitations to fall into the arms of my Beloved Companion and Helpmeet, finding provision for my every need.

Explore and share

A year or so ago, a friend, determined to make of her widowhood a spiritual journey, formed a prayer that has helped her exit the desert of dry bones. It's a prayer that today still continues to transform her. "God, I want to let go of the why did this have to happen—and move to— how are You using [widowhood] to bring me closer to You?"

Exercise 7:1

What would happen if we all pray my friend's prayer? Certainly, it would make of our widowhood a pilgrimage.

Read Psalm 84:5-7

- How does verse five advise we set our hearts?
- What promises does this passage give to the committed sojourner?

Exercise 7:2

To set our hearts on pilgrimage is to fix our heart on steadfastly seeking God; to make our seeking God our top priority.

Read Psalm 105:4

- How often are we to actively seek God?

Read Deuteronomy 4:29

- What is the promise to those who diligently seek the Divine in all things?

Exercise 7:3

Read Isaiah 54:4-5

In this passage, directed toward widows, God speaks regarding our pilgrimage. Let's listen.
- What direction does God give us in verse four?
- Review again verse five. How does God ask us to view the Divine's role in walking our pilgrimage with us?

***

Any widow's metamorphosis from loss to new life is nothing short of a miracle. Heeding the prompting of the Spirit, we rise from the senselessness of loss we have voiced in widow's desert. Our bones now firm and wearing new skin, our soul revived, infused with the breath of the Spirit, we know something of resurrection's power and hope.

However, in taking the next step, setting our minds on spiritual pilgrimage, making our life's priority seeking God, we again recognize a truth that speaks continual joy and hope to our widowed heart: we do not walk this journey alone, but in the company of our lifetime Companion—God.

So, it is, as widows, once more we find ourselves confirming what is becoming concrete truth to ourselves. Our loss is not all about loss—it's really about what we have to gain.

Prayer Suggestions

How has the Spirit prompted you today through this study or through your seeking God? Use this prayer time as a moment to respond to what you have heard God speak to your heart. Pray to live mindful of God's beloved companionship with you at all times.

CHAPTER 8

Just Do It—Pray

"Then they remembered that God was their rock, and the Most
High God their Redeemer."

Psalm 78:35

As much as I loved William and grieved his death after
he passed, at times, anger spewed into my grief. He had
left me strapped with a warehoused sized task—a job
he had postponed doing.

Seven years prior to his death, the two of us, newly married,
purchased a house in the country. Moving my belongings to it
was a cinch, but not so with William's things. Before we could
relocate his possessions, having determined our basement inad-
equate to store all his things, we added on an oversized garage.
Then we began the long process of traveling to Maryland's East-
ern Shore to retrieve William's things housed in half of a musty
old warehouse building.

He had rented the space for years. The largest section of it
served as his workshop. Sprawled out across its saw-dusted plank

flooring sat William's heavy-duty woodshop machinery, equipment he used to build beautiful handcrafted-custom furniture for clients. In the warehouse's smaller rooms and in its assorted lofts, sat his myriad of personal effects; his mass of collections and paraphernalia, all revealing his past/present, numerous hobbies and interests; and furniture inherited from his mother, the pieces now aged and mildewed with time.

Once we had it all moved into our place, William, then newly-retired, casually mentioned, he *might* now have time to sort through and downsize his bevy of stuff. I would learn in time, that William had difficulty parting with any item he owned. So of course, when his life ran out of time, everything remained just where he had put it.

As I pondered ways to approach the job, a house went on the market in the city where my children lived. I bought it. Although it needed a lot of work, the house seemed a God-send, a way to escape living alone in a rural area where I had no family, and few friends.

Naturally, in purchasing the city house, I desired a quick sale of the country home. Unfortunately, though, it was in no shape to list, due to William's bevy. I was at a loss. *What to do with it all?*

I had no spare storage at my new house, and the things William's son might have had interest in were few. The dilemma of my husband's belongings combined with packing my belongings to relocate, plus working at my new house readying it for occupancy, took its toll on me. At night, I got little rest. The dark silence stirred my grief. My heart, trying to cope with sorrow, and my mind, working overtime, relentlessly searching for and finding new things to add to my already colossal to-do list, robbed me of precious sleep.

With all that going on, being mindful of things spiritual was at best, hit-and-miss. The notion of making my widowhood a spiritual pilgrimage had not yet arrived on my radar screen. Consequently, I unconsciously had placed God in the backseat, with me in the driver's seat.

One particularly stressful day, burdened with what seemed ever-growing responsibility, total fatigue washed over me. Weary of trying to stay on top of things, emotionally stretched, my faith merely flickering, my woes claiming victory over hope, I sat in my car knowing something had to give. I was running myself ragged, going in circles. I feared for my health and wellbeing.

I thought briefly about praying, but I had neither the energy nor the presence of mind to form dedicated words. I argued, *how can I pray when my spirit feels weak...when I've not kept in touch with God? How can I pray in faith—when hope is absent and faith seems out-of-service?*

Interestingly, a thought arose from deep within me. I recognized it as the Spirit's voice, still and small, yet powerful enough to be heard over the waves of anxiety loudly colliding inside my head. In just three words, the Spirit answered my how-can-I-pray question, "Just do it."

I recognized in that moment a truth. No one longing for hope can afford *not* to pray. I was to pray in spite of my uncertainties, my fatigue, and despair. I was to pray regardless of my spiritual self-assessment score, or the way I felt emotionally. The instructions were clear—*just do it!*

I responded simply, repeating the only word I could muster in that moment, "Help...help...help..." It wasn't much of a prayer, but it proved more than enough, reawakening a hunger for God, stirring within me hope, and giving me faith. I knew at that moment, I would survive my woes.

Speaking of woes, Ecclesiastes 4:9a, 10 reads, "Two are better than one...for if they fall, one will lift up [the other]. But woe to the [one] who is alone..." It sounds as if the author knew something about the woes that befall a survivor following a loss.

"Woe to the [one] who is alone," is a haunting statement that a widow is highly likely to agree with at times, especially early on in her widowhood journey, when the woes of widowhood seem to keep coming, each one daunting. Describing a woe of widowhood, is to define it simply as any problem, event, or situation that *adds* to the widow's grief and/or *accentuates* the hardships she already experiences in living spouseless.

When woes make an appearance, to a widow struggling to hold things together, they can appear giant-sized, and of course, threatening. They instantly grab our full attention—ensnare us—demanding we concentrate on the dilemma besetting us until we resolve it. Ultimately, in such times, as often happens when our focus is zeroed in on problems, God can seem light years away, definitely not an ever-present reality. We're left then with an anemic faith drained of hope, and that, unfortunately, can induce mild-to-severe spiritual amnesia—a forgetfulness of who God really *is*. Sadly, our failed memory sabotages the motivation to pray. Thankfully though, when our prayers go silent, the Spirit begins putting suggestions in our head, ideas we think are our own —*maybe I should pray*.

The beautiful truth is that prayer and envisioning God work together. Even our tiniest prayer accomplishes much, opening our heart to the movement of God. Accordingly, every time we pray, we encounter divine benevolence!

Sometimes I view prayer as I do my eyeglasses. The first thing I do when I wake in the morning is grab my glasses. Without them, everything is a blur. That's how it goes with prayer. Without it, our spiritual vision is too blurred to see much, but through the lens of prayer, our vision is 20/20, and we are fully able to see clearly who our benevolent God is. In that light, our woes lose their threat.

Explore and share

Exercise 8:1

Ponder on this for a moment. What might happen in our personal lives if every time a woe has us fixated on our troubles we would consider it a golden opportunity to employ prayer?

- How might our prayers affect our attitude; our hope; our faith?
- How might our prayers influence our perception of who God is?

Exercise 8:2

Read Psalm 34:2-10

In this reading, David speaks his intention to bless and praise God. He gives his listeners an invitation saying something like this, "Let's take a close look at what happened when I prayed. You'll see the results—they magnify God—and they will make you want to praise God along with me!"

- How did God perform in response to David's prayers?
- What characteristics of God's nature are revealed in the ways the Divine answered David's cries?
- In what similar ways have you seen God move in your life in response to your prayers?

Exercise 8:3

Praying opens our "remembrances" of God, giving us fresh hope and knowledge that God remains with us.

- As their remembrance of the Divine re-awakens, in what symbolic way do the repentant people in today's Scripture verse (Psalm 78:35) envision God?

Read Psalm 63:6-7

- What does David remember as he is meditating on his bed?
- Ponder or discuss a time when, in prayer, you recalled an act of God on your behalf. How did that remembrance inspire fresh hope within you regarding whatever you were facing at that time?

***

Prayers are powerful. They release us from anxiety, they reset our faith and update our hope, and they give us a fresh perspective. Through the lens of prayer, our troubles, that yesterday loomed gigantic and threatening, now appear smaller; manageable. Best of all, prayer cures us of spiritual amnesia. Our eyes open as if for the first time.

We remember once more who God truly is—God is not a distant entity—but our traveling Companion, who listens to our every prayer with open ears. Our hearts jump in joyful recognition, because "Woe to the [one] who is alone" no longer applies.

Prayer suggestions

When you feel at a loss for words, pray the words of the Lord's Prayer (Luke 11:2-4). Or pray what David voiced in Psalm 27:11, "Teach me Your way, O Lord..." or his words from Psalm 6:2, "Have mercy on me, O Lord..." End your prayer time rejoicing, echoing the Palmist's remembrance, "The LORD lives! Praise be to my Rock!" (2 Samuel 22:47 NIV).

CHAPTER 9

Hope for a Family Unglued

"My hope...uprooted like a tree."

Job19:10b

As often is the case when death invades, stealing one parent and leaving the other, the empty chair at the dinner table is disconcerting. The vacancy speaks a message to each family member, "Things have changed—and now, so must you."

I recalled that thought when a newly widowed, long-time friend called me to say, "Do you remember how, years ago, your family fell apart after your husband John died? That's what's happening to my family in the wake of my husband's loss."

As every widow knows well, unwilled change such as loss, turns one's world upside down, uprooting everything, commanding that we "let go" of the old so that we might embrace the new—a 'new' we have not asked for nor want. The old was fine just the way it was!

However, change that follows loss pays no heed to our wishes. It insists we turn our backs on the past; that we surrender many of our hopes and dreams; that we forfeit relationships of those who, feeling uncomfortable with our loss, withdraw their friendship from us. What we may find the hardest to relinquish though, is to give up, to let go, of our family unit as it once was, prior to loss.

That was true of me when John died. He had been a hard worker, an excellent provider, a dad whose eyes twinkled with joy when he played with our children. However, he was also controlling and demanding. Questioning or contradicting his ideas generally brought out the worst in him. His ire would flame, scorching us, the family he loved.

Fear of overstepping John's authority had shaped our family. His laws kept the children and I bound through the years, restricting our behaviors, obviously making us co-dependent at times. Sadly, keeping John's rules often silenced our true selves that lay somewhere lost deep within our beings. However, when he died, the control—the aged, dried adhesive with which he kept us in place—splintered into chips, leaving us a family unglued. Suddenly unbound, the control structure gone, we were released to seek our own desires, to speak freely, and to explore who we were as individuals.

Naturally, in a family of five females finally given permission to speak their mind freely, it's easy to understand that our family relationships took a nosedive! Often, we stood at odds with one another, verbally lashing out. Our relationships suffered when, unhappy with the changes we saw in each other, we complained about this one or that one, "Why can't she just be who she always was? I liked her old self better!"

All of us struggled in this time of change. Most of my children, confounded by the new behaviors they saw in me, sought to understand me. *She's not the mom we used to have!* I grieved, unable to comprehend why they couldn't grasp my need to pursue a new life. Our struggling set the stage for further family division; on one side stood those unhappy with me, on the other stood children trying to support me, with me smack-dab in the middle.

It was tragically sad. The family we once had been now lay in ruins. We were a mess.

Those upset with me, out of frustration, like parents of a wayward teenager, sought to reign me in—to reason with me—to make me come into alignment with the old me. The children who were supportive didn't agree with that approach. The rift grew into a large chasm.

My heart bled. Of course, I felt rejection but my sorrow far outweighed that. My family was broken and I was the cause! Guilt became my middle name, a name full of blame that I would wear for years.

Desperate to see my family restored, with an *I-can-fix-this* attitude, I sat about to glue my family back together—so we could be as we had been in the past.

Sadly, my attempts to mend things and bring the family back together, only tore us farther apart. It seemed no matter what I did, my actions produced pain, deepening my children's heartache and widening the chasm dividing my family into two camps.

There came a point in time, when weary of me and my determination to fix the family, one of the camps said, "ENOUGH." They had given up trying to figure me out, to save me from myself, to spare me from making mistakes.

I can't imagine how painful that step was for them to take. They had lost their father—and now me. The "Mom" they had known as children, in their eyes, had expired. Now, the only thing they wanted from me was distance. Their request for it broke my heart. My hope for a reunited family seemed as today's scripture says, "uprooted like a tree."

When I remarried, and moved to my new husband's home in the mid-west, my children got the distance they wanted, but for me it meant greater sorrow. Every day I grieved the close-knit relationships I once knew with my daughters. *Would I ever know their love and favor again?* One day as I sat crying, I sensed the Divine challenging me with an invitation, "Let go of your family."

"HOW?" I asked, rationalizing it an impossible task. I heard a reply, "Give things time."

For the next two years, slowly, I learned the secret of letting go of my family. For me personally, it would take patience. It would require my honoring my children's request for space, and it would involve daily "connecting" with my family members through praying prayers of healing, restoration and blessings on them. In time I would see God answer those prayers.

Explore and share

Whenever I reflect on those long-ago years when my family became unglued, I see that time of learning to "let go" as one of my first major steps of transformation. My "letting go" freed not only me, but my children. The years of separation gave God leeway to mend what only God could "fix."

Exercise 9:1

Your story may bear similarities to mine, or it may not. One thing for certain though, loss influences our relationships, either enriching them—or for a season—disrupting them. One gives us hope and the second has us praying for hope. What is your story?

Ponder the questions below and journal your response. If in a group, share together your answers.

- How did your loss affect your family members? In what ways did your loss reform or transform your relationships as a family?
- In what ways did your loss alter or influence your friendships—to include groups of friends you and your husband knew as couples?
- Are there any relationships that changed to the extent that you have had to release them? Where are you in that process?

Exercise 9:2

Much of our battle to let go is a result of desperately trying to hold on to yesterday. Therein is the beauty of letting go. It creates space for God to work, to bring into being what the Divine has yet planned for our lives, giving us hope for a future that we cannot yet imagine.

Letting go doesn't mean, like some may mistakenly think, that we have to rid our homes of everything that reminds us of our deceased spouse. It only means to remain sensitive, alert to anything now and in the future, that we discover may emotionally be tethering our hearts to the past, preventing us from moving fully into wholeness.

Take a moment to search your heart. Consider carefully and honestly. *Presently, is there anything holding me back?* Use the list below as a starting point to stir your thinking.
- My family?
- A relationship that I know is not truly the best for me?
- Something I'm attached to that keeps me excessively tied to my grief, to the past?
- Other?

Exercise 9:3

Read Isaiah 43: 18-19 & Philippians 3:13

In this verse, Isaiah gives us a mini-lesson in letting go, a lesson helpful to any widow.
- What does the verse tell us to forget?
- What does it recommend we look for?
- What does the reading in Philippians suggest we forget?
- What does it recommend we reach for?

***

Today, when I look at my children, I see a family transformed. We are not—nor will we ever be—perfect. Like all families, we differ and we have our raw moments ever calling us to further transformation. What is new though, in our family, is the thing that holds us together. It's called grace; God's bonding agent. Grace that helps us continue to let go of each other, freeing God to shape us individually according to Heaven's plan and time-table. This amazing glue, sweet grace, is keeping our family's tree deeply rooted in love, its branches revealing hope in full bloom.

Prayer suggestions

Pray to behold God as the fixer, the transformer of hearts. Pray for God to continually transform you and your family, so that all members might live in wholeness. Pray for strength and courage to let go of anything holding you back from moving forward.

CHAPTER 10

Hope that Waits

"For I know the thoughts I think toward you, says the Lord, thoughts of peace and not of evil, to give you a future and a hope."

Jeremiah 29:11

"Please take a drink of water," I said standing at William's bedside two weeks prior to his passing. His fluid intake had decreased drastically causing me concern.

As I moved the drinking straw toward his lips, William resolutely zipped them closed. I tried twice again, pleading, "Please take at least a sip."

When I coaxed him for the fourth time, his abrupt response caught me off guard. Although weak and frail, his old brawn made an appearance. His arm strong, he pushed away my hand with a loud "WAIT!" Then, his eyes narrowed into slits. He studied me dubiously, as if questioning my motives.

What he said next; I will never forget: "I'm suspicious of you and of what's in that glass..."

Shocked, I stood there fighting tears. Throughout our sweet seven-year marriage, William had never questioned my loyalty or my love. I told myself his irrational thinking was a result of his heavy medication, but it didn't help. My heart broke to see him think of me as untrustworthy and deceitful.

I felt, in that moment, that I had just lost yet another piece of my husband—his trust. I stroked his forehead gently, hoping my touch would revive love's memory, and mend the connection of trust that had kept us one.

My hand lingering on his brow, doing my best to ignore the lump in my throat, I spoke slowly. It was important that he remember the truth. "Oh Honey, don't you know? I would never hurt you. I love you so much. How could I do you *any* harm?"

His gaze remained fixed on me, his eyes still reading distrust. I left the room with William's words piecing my heart repeatedly, *"I'm suspicious of you... "*

A few hours later, unable to forget the hurtful words, a sense of Holy Presence comforted me whispering, "I know your pain and sadness."

A moment later, I heard the Spirit speak again, the Voice this time tinged with great sorrow. "The way you feel about losing William's trust describes how I feel when you turn suspicious of Me. Like when you question what I am doing in your life... or why I have allowed certain things to happen. Or those times when you feel I've been unfair, withholding from you what you feel you need. It deeply pains me to see you judging My motives and intentions as evil.

"My child," the Spirit continued, softly echoing the very words I had spoken to William. *"Don't you know? I would never hurt you. I love you so much. How could I do you any harm?"*

The thought that I had viewed God with such distrust shocked and grieved me, but I knew it was true. My life's history of loss and troubles had left me wary of life—untrusting of it.

I had often looked at God as the Author of my life's story like the Psalmist viewed his life's story. "And in Your book, they all were written, the days fashioned for me, when as yet there were none of them" (Psalm 139:16b). Nevertheless, I had to face the truth.

I did not fully trust God's authorship, nor did I applaud it.

I owned a propensity toward God suspicions. Proof of that was a subtle dread that haunted me continually: *when and what will be the next tragedy recorded on the pages of my life, telling of something else precious taken from me?*

I understood that day that I had to change. To know hope along my journey, I would need to lay down my fears and doubts—but how?

Gradually, since William's passing, I have come to believe that there are various kinds of hope, some types effective, others not so much when it comes to helping widows like myself to lay down our God suspicions and fears.

For instance, one kind of hope is Wishful Hope, the type I was accustomed to having. Wishful Hope is self-manufactured. It lives in the thought, "I hope things turn out well so I can have a happy life." Such hope is dependent on one's moods, or life's circumstances, and is prone to anxiety, making it weak and undependable when most needed.

Then there's the Day-Lily variety of hope. It has shallow roots. Unable to withstand life's harshness, it wilts almost immediately.

A few years ago, I met a widow whose hope seemed like that— the Day-Lily assortment—hope present for an hour at best, then gone. Many caring people tried to help, speaking hope and direction to her but she would immediately reply, "Yes, but you don't understand. Every time my life seems to come together, something negative comes along and takes my happiness away again."

It was tragic. No one, not pastors, counselors, or friends, could talk her out of her notion. A dark cloak of hopelessness clung to her, clouding her thinking and her existence, leaving her believing God had no better plan for her life than trouble.

I wish she could have found what I see as Hope that Waits. It's the opposite of Wishful Hope, and it bears no resemblance to Day-Lily-Hope. It's hope that is effective in helping anyone lay down God suspicions and fears.

Hope that Waits is not self-manufactured; it is not based on circumstances, and it has nothing to do with one's mood. It does not need the sun to thrive. To the contrary, Hope that Waits, in the dark hours of adversity, proves most resilient.

This organic variety of hope remains lively, radical, constant, and infinite, made so because its source comes from the gift of Christ living within us as *living* hope (1 Peter 1:3). This living hope flows like a mighty river through our inward being, exalting the Triune God, giving us the capacity *to wait restfully in complete trust in God*. Waiting, resting and trusting is what Hope that Waits looks like in action.

Practicing Hope that Waits begins, naturally with waiting on the movement of God. Especially in today's age where instant gratification is often the goal, we may quickly notice we haven't the patience or desire to wait. However, Living Hope streaming within us, gives us the ability to learn to "tarry," as a past generation called the act of waiting.

Learning to wait on God takes intentional practice. It asks that we move from a stressful mindset to a restful thought life so that we might live restful with a quiet heart—the perfect soil in which to grow trust.

Of course, no one is born with absolute trust in God. Seeds of trust lie in all of us, but to mature them takes putting Hope that Waits in action, consistently practicing its process of waiting, resting, and trusting in all circumstances and situations. Gradually, we come to see the fruit of our practicing. Free of God suspicions, now, perhaps for the first time, we *genuinely* believe what God has declared to us. "For I know the plans I have for you...

plans to prosper you and not to harm you, plans to give you hope and a future" (Jeremiah 29:11 NIV).

Explore and Share

David said, "Oh taste and see that the Lord is good..." (Psalm 34:8). Waiting on God, calling our minds and hearts to rest, and trusting in God, lets us sample what David tasted: God's goodness. Its divine taste lingering on our lips, it's not uncommon to hear ourselves making a bold statement of faith. *Although I cannot possibly see how things are going to work out, no matter the outcome, I trust God that that some good will evolve from my loss— from my present pain.*

However, life being life, and our hearts fickle at times, it is possible to unconsciously slack off practicing Hope that Waits. It becomes evident to us when fears and God suspicions start to sneak back in eating away trust; when our soul is not at rest making waiting on God impossible, and when our awareness of the Living Hope existing within us seems less acute.

What to do in such times? Let's explore some options in the exercises below.

Exercise 10:1

Read Isaiah 30:15

- Ponder or discuss the steps God speaks in this verse. How can we walk them out? How might they help us in times when we are not fully convinced that God is doing what is in our best interest?

Read Psalm 42:11

- How does the Psalmist's talking to his soul in this verse illustrate a soul-talking pattern we can use when our soul is not at rest?

Exercise 10:2

Read Psalm 27:13-14

When we find our God-confidence is lacking...
- What steps does David recommend in the above Scriptures?

Exercise 10:3

This exercise opens our heats to God's love, enabling us to effectively practice Hope that Waits.

Read Zephaniah 3:17

- Listen to its words as they were meant to be heard—a personal love from God to you.
- Write down what you hear. Keep your notes where you can ponder them often.

***

The joy of continually practicing Hope that Waits, waiting, resting, trusting, is that it keeps us delightfully conscious of Christ, our Living Hope dwelling within us, saving us, redeeming us, blessing us with a dynamic awareness of God's unconditional, eternal love. It is—Living Hope—that opens our ears to hear God whisper to our hearts, "It's very important that you know the truth. Yours is going to be a marvelous story! You'll see that I have planned only the best for you. I love you so very much—I could never do you harm."

Prayer suggestions

Pray to remain faithful to practice waiting on God. Pray for a quiet mind, for a soul that knows how to rest while waiting on God. Pray for an open, trusting heart toward God. Thank God for Christ, the Living Hope dwelling within you.

Chapter 11

When There's No End in Sight— Cling!

"Cling to what is good."
Romans 12:9

After William's death, I finally placed our home on the market, and was overjoyed when within a short time, I received an acceptable offer. With the house now under contract, I could dedicate my time and efforts fully to the cleanup and restoration of the house to where I had relocated.

No longer would I need to make weekly trips out to the old place to check on it, and to mow and maintain its five acres. It had been a bi-weekly chore William and I had shared together. I had found doing it solo was grueling work. Nevertheless, with a contract in hand, I was free of all that now.

Unfortunately, the buyers, within weeks of closing on the property, reneged. The burden of the homestead's upkeep came crashing down, weighing on my shoulders again. The present real-estate slump did not give me much hope. My long drives to the property resumed; I filled the travel time with prayers for a new buyer.

One evening, at home in my new place, I watched a movie. The storyline included a stressed-out man repeatedly complaining of his many problems to a listening friend. His friend replied, "Look, in the end things will turn out okay, and if they don't, you are not at the end yet."

The next morning with the line from the movie playing in my head, I left home to make the drive over the mountains, back to the homestead. My heart grieving William's absence, and my whole being despairing from the weight of carrying both the physical and financial load of owning two properties—with no sign of that changing in the near future—*I wondered, will 'the end' ever come for me, bringing closure to this chapter of my life?* My exhausted body posed another question. *How long can I go on like this, doing the workload of two by myself?*

Exasperated, I moaned aloud, "God, do you understand that all this is too much for me? Are You aware that I'm not young anymore?"

My words were more a complaint than a question—but right then, while waiting at a traffic light, I noticed a billboard on the side of the road. A portion of it loomed large reading, *"Believe and achieve."*

My heart stopped for a second. The traffic signal turned green. I drove on, but the uncanniness of the sighting and the sign's message left me on alert. The word "believe" in particular had grabbed my attention. *Was that God speaking to me?*

My tired mind and fatigued body refused another challenge. They begged me to consider the billboard's cliché for what it was; a business advertisement. However—in case—the words were God sent, I prayed. *God, I don't understand. Just what is it that you want me to believe?*

A flash of movement to the left caught my eye. Outside, on the windshield, I saw a small, dried-brown leaf fluttering toward my car's antenna where it attached itself. The edges of the little leaf looked like arms clinging to a pole—holding on for dear life.

Amazingly, I watched it fight the wind—and win. As if glued to the antenna, it refused to let go.

The perfect timing of the leaf's arrival, plus watching it cling relentlessly to the antenna, seemed a sacred moment, touching my heart and bringing tears to my eyes. At that moment, I considered the billboard's reading and the little leaf appearing as God's way of encouraging me to cling to faith's pole. I needed that encouragement as much of the time my "believing" was not faith-based but on what I saw and judged with my human eyes (reasoning), leaving me continually overwhelmed, falling far short of what I wished to achieve.

In retrospect, I now consider that day's events as related to an earlier date—the day I watched the coroner wheel William's lifeless body out of our home. Afterward, standing in the eerie silence, acutely sensing a cavern of emptiness within me, fear washed over me. What if that emptiness remained? I quickly prayed. *Oh God, my desire is for You to please fill the void of William's sweet presence with a genuine and abundant sense of Your presence. May Your company with me be as unmistakably vivid and real as William's physical company was.*

In remembering that prayer, I think how ironical that a few months after praying it, I would *happen by* the billboard, read its words—and then seconds later, a little leaf would *happen* to fly by and catch itself on my car's antenna, sticking there like glue in spite of blowing winds.

Today I still recognize that incident as a sacred encounter with God, but had I known then what I know today, I would have interpreted it differently. I would have viewed it as God speaking, saying to me, "I heard your prayer the day William passed. You will see it answered as you learn to cling to Me as tenaciously as that leaf clung to your car. You perform this clinging by *believing in what you cannot see* with your physical eyes. Always remember, believing is a choice. Choose to believe with every fiber of your being in the reality of My company living within and with you, and it will bring to you your desire to know My presence as vividly as you knew William's physical presence."

Explore and share

God's presence with us *is* genuine reality, but, unfortunately, for many of us, glimmers of that truth often only comes home to roost when we are sitting in a house of worship feeling a fresh wave of the Spirit's movement.

However, there are those who believingly cling to the Spiritual Actuality of God-Within, readily recognizing the Divine's "divine" company residing with them, giving them a vivid consciousness of a Holy Energy flowing through them. The Apostle Paul was such a person. Living with this mighty Energy coursing through him, he said, "I can do all things through Christ who strengthens me" (Philippians 4:13).

Let's begin our exploration, first seeking the base point at which we can start to genuinely believe with all our heart in the actual existence of God within us.

Exercise 11:1

One thing that can keep us blinded to God's presence within is spiritual self-judgements. They may cause us to esteem ourselves as unworthy of God's attendance, or not righteous enough to live in the Divine's company. Such spiritual lies can cause us to try and hide from God like Adam and Eve unsuccessfully attempted to do. Sadly, spiritual falsehoods telling us we cannot measure up to God's favor definitely curtail desire for God's company and cause us to doubt God's love for us.

Since self-judgements hold us distanced from God, let's look in the Holy Scriptures. They always invite us to see ourselves in God's mirror, a looking glass that reveals the fallacy of any imperfect reasoning by confirming our dearness to God.

Read John 3:16-17 and John 15:1-5

In this reading from John, Jesus gently opens our spirit's eyes with a parable permitting us to see exactly how God views us declaring us, completely qualified—spiritually approved to dwell in the Divine's company. Throughout this passage, let's carefully note the numerous times Jesus declares that He is the "Vine."

- According to John 3:16-17, why did God provide this Christ Vine?
- How do we see the outworking of God's Salvation's plan in what Christ says to His followers in John 15:3?
- In John 15:5, what does Jesus call those who cling to the Vine ("abide" in Him)?

In verse four, Jesus says that a branch can do nothing on its own, confirming that on our own merit, yes, we are unworthy. However, as branches drawing life from the Holy Vine, mercy and redemption flowing through our veins, we live as Vine-clingers. We grace God's beautiful vineyard, each branch precious, cared for, growing, and producing good fruit. That describes you, me—all who actively cleave to the Christ-Vine.

From this place of belonging, we need only to open our soul to see that we are beyond all doubt spiritually positioned in God's presence. Now it's up to us to exercise the awareness of our position, in order to actively immerse ourselves in the marvelous Reality of God in and with us.

Exercise 11:2

Many of us have followed good spiritual disciplines throughout our lives, reading Scriptures, praying, attending church, but at the end of the day, in our widowhood when we need it most we still may find ourselves without a genuine sense of the Divine's Aliveness with and within us.

If you find yourself in that state, as I and others have experienced, it's helpful to consider this: believingly clinging to the Divine Presence is all about transferring our accumulated head knowledge of God's love, faithfulness, and goodness, to our hearts and letting it dwell there as realism. It takes mindfulness, practice, and discipline, but in striving to consciously live in the authenticity of God's company, we see amazing results. Our spiritual practices of old continue, but now they seem as if highly energized, igniting within us constant new understandings, fueling us with fresh desire and love for God—and expanding within us compassion and love for others.

Read Ephesians 3:19-20

Reflect quietly for a moment. Try to grasp a fuller comprehension of Paul's powerful description in verse twenty of Christ's dynamic power.

- Where does Paul say that power is now and will always remain at work?
- How does such a truth stir your heart?

Exercise 11:3

It's wise to realize that, unfortunately, at times, the thought of God dwelling in us can be stalemated by our human thinking and our logic. Logic keeps our eyes glued only on the here-and-now facts. Our spiritual eyes close at such times, and suddenly, living in the actual Presence of the Highest just seems no more than abstract thought. When this happens, once again, we need to reacquaint ourselves with certain Scriptures that can reawaken us to Reality, and use our spiritual imagination to envision God walking alongside us, living in us.

Read Colossians 1:27 and Ephesians 2:22

- How do these Scriptures affirm that God dwelling in us is reality?
- How might we employ our spiritual imagination to help us recognize the truth of God's presence with us?

Eugene H. Peterson, author of The Message Bible, says, "For Christians, whose largest investment is in the invisible, the imagination is indispensable."[1]

Every day we use imagination. When we dress for work, we make our clothing choice imagining how we will look in that item. When we prepare a new recipe, we imagine its taste. When we read a book, we imagine our self in the places and situations the story presents.

God, the author of imagination, created the world with it. As entities created in God's image, the imagination gene has been passed on to us! God's Word, the Holy Bible, spreads out a feast of delicious imagery, inviting us to sample it, "to taste" God's richness with our imagination.

Imagination opens our spiritual eyes to see the analogy put forth in Scriptures, passages that offer us a "visual" revealing of God's character, and God's movement within us. For instance, the Song of Solomon invites us in chapter two to see the Divine in this light, "Like an apple tree...In his shade I take pleasure in sitting, and his fruit is sweet to my taste" (Song of Songs 2: 3 CEB). Another example is when the prophet Isaiah calls us to reach Godward and sense God's hand holding ours (Isaiah 41:13). Indeed, imagination illuminates God's written Word, giving us countless opportunities to interact, to engage with the God who is dwelling with us and loves to fellowship with us.

***

The Spirit is constantly giving opportunities for us to know the living, breathing reality of God within us. Each opportunity invites us to engage with God, encounters that move us ever deeper into intimate union with the Divine, symbolic of the merger Jesus prayed for on our behalf in John 17:21.

Love runs deep in this holy marriage of Soul and soul. Communicating and communing together, often just for the pure pleasure of being together, it's not long before this holy togetherness is indeed the Reality in which we live, move and have our being (Acts 17:18).

It's a union profitable to any widow. It gives her the desire of her heart: companionship of Someone who dearly and deeply loves her unconditionally. Even when there seems no end in sight to her troubles, cleaving to her Companion, she knows eternal hope, eternal love.

Prayer suggestions

Take a moment to dedicate your imagination to God. Pray for God to help you to keep it unsullied from misuse. There is no end to knowing the Realty of God dwelling in us. Accordingly, pray continually to move into deeper union with the Divine.

CHAPTER 12

That Thing Called Loneliness

"God is doing what is best for us, training us to live God's holy best."

(Hebrews 12:10b MSG)

"I should have known better, but he was helpful, funny, smart, handsome, and encouraging—and I was lonely," says my friend, a widow of eight years, speaking of dating a man who, although there were indications all along, after three years, rejected her.

Her words "I was lonely" names the bane of widowhood: that *thing* called loneliness—a hollow dry abyss within, always crying for satisfaction, commanding its host to quench its thirst.

The widow, in seeking to gratify that demand, can find that her efforts to satisfy loneliness' thirst may leave her with a list of 'I-should-have-know-better' regrets. I have such a list myself, as do many widows struck down by loneliness.

Of course, loneliness is a normal part of life. It's inclusive, visiting everybody occasionally. On its arrival, one can only hope it will not stay long. However, regarding the widow's brand of loneliness, especially in early days of widowhood, it demands an extended stay, moving into her heart, uninvited, of course. It begins to dominate her life. Wherever she goes, loneliness tags along, stalking her. Returning to her home, she walks through the door hoping loneliness remained outside—but there it is—its gloomy presence waiting to greet her.

There's a definitive aspect of a widow's loneliness that sets it apart from standard loneliness. It's called *aloneness*. Acute and desperate, aloneness magnifies loneliness' whine, giving it a mocking tongue, that taunts a widow unmercifully, reminding her how empty of love her life is. "Look around you...you have *no one*—no soul-mate, no one to hold your hand, to share your bed, to kiss, to commune with...."

As if that's not enough, it insists on pronouncing to the widow a dooming life-sentence: *Loveless and alone—so shall you spend the rest of your days.*

Most certainly, the widow's loneliness owns great power. It births a terrible restlessness, stirring within her a hunger for anything this world offers that might arrest loneliness. She sets out on a quest looking for something to do...or a somebody to love, to discover whatever it is that will set her heart free of loneliness and feed her what she has lost; a spouse's admiration, the delightful taste of communion and love, the sweet essence of life and living.

Unfortunately, captive to loneliness, its restlessness can drive a widow, keeping her in a continual search mode. Hungry for companionship, she may seek out relationships, and to avoid time alone, she may find herself bouncing from one activity to another in order to stay busy, always looking for tangible things to satisfy her. Regretfully, most times, in the end all the "some-things" and "somebodies" she latches onto seem to be but a temporary fix, proving disappointingly short of what she had hoped to find.

Sadly, her endless searching for satisfaction grows as futile as the action of a caged hamster, spinning on its toy-wheel going nowhere but round-and-round. Living in such a mode steals her energy, denies her hope, stalls her healing, all of which distance her from her overall objective: to know a genuine new beginning where she will live in wholeness.

Most, if not all of us, can see pieces of ourselves in today's reading, leaving us wondering, where is hope found in the midst of that thing called loneliness? Can we actually triumph over loneliness, and tame the restlessness it pours into our hearts?

Yes, if and when we factor God into the equation.

Explore and share

Quite honestly, my first time widowed, I found no hope in my loneliness, but then, how could I? Even though I had faith in God, I just couldn't stretch it far enough to believe, that God, or even praying to God, was "big" enough to arrest my intense loneliness. I figured that appeasing loneliness was my job, not God's. The result of fighting loneliness on my own created for me a hefty-sized list of 'I-should-have-know-better regrets'.

However, in remembering the futility of that unwise behavior, after William passed, I did an about-face. I considered God my *only* hope. Seeing prayer as my spiritual lifeline, I sincerely believed prayer would help my loneliness, but I wasn't thoroughly convinced as to what extent. I wondered, *Can God's grace completely satisfy my lonely heart?*

Having determined that I would make of my widowhood a spiritual pilgrimage, I looked to the Divine to answer that question. Today's Scripture reads, "God is doing what is best for us, training us to live God's holy best." I figured, since loneliness and I were thrown together, that I would consider it as part of God's training program. Much of my training would consist of making decisions to allow God, not me, to choose what was best for me.

How did those decisions affect my loneliness? How might allowing God to choose the best for you, affect your loneliness?

Sometimes I saw amazing results. Loneliness would hit me afresh like a ton of bricks. I would react by praying for grace and strength to endure, for steadfastness to stay away from reaching out to anything but God's best for me. Many of those prayers brought almost instant relief, leaving me awed that God's power could touch my loneliness. In those times of answered prayer, I felt divinely loved, comforted, safe—and delightedly satisfied.

However, I knew other times when my holding fast in prayer did *not* result in instant help, days when I would awaken with loneliness gnawing on my insides, screaming for satisfaction, expecting me to feed it something tangible. I recall entertaining various notions to appease my loneliness in those desperate times, but knowing I hadn't succeeded the first time with similar plans, why take a chance on erring again? So, I learned, on difficult days, times when grace and strength to endure seemed worlds away, to pray because—if nothing else—it kept loneliness from driving me mad—and my restlessness from running wild.

Of course, I still have occasional moments where I may want to skip God's latest training session on how to stay atop loneliness. My head tells me *to take a class break, yes, you're human, but surely you can trust yourself to appease your current loneliness.* My mind chimes in, presenting me with a plethora of perfectly logical ideas to entertain. Go *online like you did before and find a relationship...you need more activity in your life, join this or do that... or at least go shopping, buy something for yourself, it'll make you feel better. Or, here's a better idea, kick this melancholy loneliness...leave town, take a trip...*

Definitely there is nothing wrong with any of those ideas—unless—I am considering them as a method to override the loneliness that God is using to train me to know God's best. Consequently, although I am not always as faithful as I want to be, I have learned to hold up my human ideas to God, then to listen. Sometimes I hear Divine approval for what I'm considering, other times I hear God saying, "If you want my best, wait on Me to bring it to you."

The truth I've gained, along with other widows, lets me say triumphantly, *"Yes, God's grace really, truly does satisfy a lonely heart!* This satisfaction is a result of God's enabling grace, and the Spirit giving me the willingness to let God choose—not simply what is good for me, but what is the very best for me—which includes a heart at rest, no longer besieged by desperate loneliness.

Exercise 12:1

In order to help ourselves to allow God to use our loneliness, we need to honestly consider our current perspective on loneliness. Of the two choices below, which one best describes your view of loneliness?

- I see loneliness more like a disease that makes me feel miserable. It requires external treatment—like doing something positive to offset it.
- I view loneliness as a cry of my heart for something deeper than any external resources can give me.

Exercise 12:2

Below are spiritual practices that God calls us to employ. We will find these practices, not only prepare our heart to receive God's holy best, but give us effective measures to deal with trials, such as loneliness.

Read Psalm 46:10a

- What does this verse invite us to practice? What knowing does it say we will gain from practicing stillness?

Read Psalm 131:2

- What step does David find effective? How might our doing the same benefit our soul in when we encounter loneliness?

Read Lamentations 3:25-26

- What practices do these verses reinforce, and why might heeding them bless us with God's holy best in times of loneliness?

Read 1 Timothy 5:5

- What practices does this call the widow to participate in daily?

Considering the practices above, when loneliness shows up, what is or will be your first response:
- To address it inwardly by practicing the above practices?
- To address it externally, immediately feeding your loneliness a happy meal of activity to quiet its restlessness?

Exercise 12:3

Read 2 Corinthians 12:8-10

- How does God's words, as spoken to Paul, speak to us regarding times when loneliness invades and persists—and we want only to be rid of its infirmity?

Read 1 Timothy 6:6

- God's holy best inevitably leads us to find great gain. According to this verse, what does this gain consist of?

***

Developing a quiet heart and listening ears, along with steadfastness in waiting on God through trust and prayer, does far more for us than just keeping us from creating a list of 'I-should-have-known-better' regrets. These practices unite our hearts with God's, filling us with fresh devotion for the Holy One. Having found delicious satisfaction in this union stirs a deep hunger to keep growing through our spiritual practices. Eventually, in our continued practice, we discover that more than anything this earth has to offer, we want God. This affirms that God's love has captured and enraptured our hearts.

That fact lets us glimpse another marvelous reward of living in "God's holy best". Through spiritual practices, we emerged as victors. Leaning on God's enabling grace and love flowing through us, loneliness loses its home. Sweet, delicious contentment moves into its space.

Prayer suggestions

Pray the Lord's Prayer (Matthew 6:9-13) daily. Pray for a quiet heart, and a discerning spirit. Pray to stand steadfast in allowing God to choose the "holy best" for you. Thank God for the victories you win over loneliness.

CHAPTER 13

God-Watching

"I will lift up my eyes...My help comes from the Lord..."

Psalm 121:1a, 2a

Winter came early in 2012, the year William passed. I hadn't lived at my new location long before a snow/ice storm swept across the area one night. Awakening in the morning, I found myself snowbound. Regretfully, I had not met any of my neighbors nor had I arranged for snowplowing service. This left me with a dilemma.

Seeing the mess outside, I checked the forecast only to learn additional snow would arrive in the evening. My mind immediately spun into high gear. *What can I do about clearing my driveway?* My garaged-car, held hostage by the ice and snow was going nowhere soon. I felt as trapped as my car—alone in an unfamiliar house—alone in a neighborhood full of strangers.

I gazed out my dining room window to study my options. I sighed. My driveway glistened like white glass. Physically, I knew the job of clearing it much too big a task for me—but a widow living alone, in a new locale—*What was I to do?*

Wishing for an immediate solution, I started talking aloud to God, suggesting *my* plan. It seemed a good one at the time. I asked God to nudge and motivate one of my children to call telling me they'd be over as soon as they dug themselves out and the roads cleared. That would solve my problem.

However, after my prayer, knowing that family members would probably have enough weather-related issues of their own to deal with, my proposed plan seemed impractical and irrational, but I could still hope, right? Accordingly, I added an addendum to my prayer. "Okay God, if the kids don't call in an hour offering their help for later today—since I don't know anyone nearby to help me—THEN I will go outside and do the job myself... And God," I added, "If it comes to that, please...please, give me strength to accomplish the task."

I took one more despairing look out the window. My heart sunk. There was no way I could manage such a feat. My only hope rested on some form of divine intervention—a miracle of some sort. "God, You could spare me; You could send an angel," I suggested. I wasn't sure what God thought about that silly notion, but I was definitely open to the idea.

An hour later, after no phone call—and no angel, I headed outside and began the task with a pickaxe and shovel. Ten minutes into my axe slinging, already exhausted, I stopped for a breather. Hearing the sound of ice splintering behind me, I turned to see a stranger at the end of my drive, chopping away at the ice, shoveling huge chunks off the driveway.

Recalling my angel request, my jaw dropped. Stunned, I stood there gaping. Could it really be? Who was the stranger intent on clearing my driveway?

My angelic visitor turned out to be human—one of the many neighbors I had not yet met. He insisted on doing the entire driveway—on the condition that I go inside and stay warm!

Why God answered my prayer in such a remarkable way still mystifies me. Possibly the reason had something to do with the practice of looking God-ward—of God-watching. From that incident, I learned something that would encourage me throughout my widowhood journey, and perhaps it will encourage you also.

This is the truth I gleaned: God-watching always brings the same results—although you never know what *form* God will appear in—it's inevitable, the Divine *will* show up in your life—"in your neighborhood"—in response to your need. For me, that winter day, God appeared in the "angelic" form of Divine Provision.

That encounter opened my eyes. How many times had evidence of God's activity shown itself in my daily life but I had missed sensing it because I was not watching for God's movement?

Quite often in the Bible, Jesus, speaking to those like me, whose eyes can get easily glazed over by life's concerns and doings, repeatedly points out the necessity of living with a conscious spiritual alertness that looks for God in all things, at all times. "Watch..., for you neither know the day nor the hour in which the Son of Man is coming" (Matthew 25:13). "Take heed, watch and pray..." (Mark 13:33).

It makes perfect sense, practicing a moment by moment alertness that is sensitive to God's presence is a holy safeguard. Consequently, the habit of God-watching—of God awareness—is a vital and worthwhile spiritual practice. It readies us, keeps us on our spiritual toes watching for Christ's coming—and it blesses us in this life with discerning eyes—able to detect God's movement in the everyday details of our lives.

Explore and share

How might embracing the practice of God-watching profit a widow? What will she find in doing it?

It seems, as widows, we're always trying to compensate, to take up the slack left to us by our deceased spouses, to perform solo, doing the work of two. This is where a healthy God-watching practice can aid the widow.

As she prays, trusts, and watches for God's provision for whatever she is facing or needs, a sacred "Something" happens. For example, an unexpected check comes in the mail, an unanticipated job opportunity surfaces, a mysterious positive change of attitude takes place within you or another, or a neighbor shows up to help with a task. Such happenings, some may call coincidence but to the widow on a spiritual pilgrimage, she recognizes them as God encounters. Each one surprises her, expands her perception of God, strengthens her faith, and magnifies hope.

Exercise 13:1

You may ask, "How will I recognize when God shows up?"

That's a good question. Have you ever driven to the airport to do a prearranged pick up of someone you've never seen? The only way you recognize the person is by the placard they hold in front of them, bearing their name.

That's how it is with God. We recognize the Divine's arrival by the placard God wears; the attributes that announce who God is. The Scriptures below give opportunity to familiarize ourselves with some of the attributes of the Divine. Therefore, when they appear in our daily lives, we will recognize them as a movement of God, as God showing up, previewing the Divine's love and affection for us.

What attributes of God do you find in these Scriptures? Record them as a means of establishing them in your mind.
- Psalm 121:5-8
- Genesis 22:14
- Jeremiah 33:6
- 2 Corinthians 9:8
- Isaiah 12:2
- 2 Corinthians 1:3-4a

Exercise 13:2

Think of an incident or a time when you have personally witnessed a God manifestation displaying one of the Divine's attributes as listed in Scriptures above. If in a group, share your God encounter and what it meant to you.

Exercise 13:3

Reflect on the question below and write out your response to it, or if comfortable doing so, share your answer with your group.
- How do you desire God to show up in your life at this present time?

Read Romans 8:31-32

- According to the above text, how many things is God willing to provide for us? Is there a limit?

As God-watchers, assured that "all things" (as per verse 32) are ours for the asking, let's consider the following question.
- What kind of a difference do you think it would make in your life if each time a need or a concern surfaced, you would pray, "God, you know my situation. You have already made provision for it. Please open my eyes to see it."

***

David is a perfect example of a genuine God-watcher. He continually saw God as his mainstay. In today's Scripture, he says, "I will lift up my eyes...My help comes from the Lord..."

Likewise, it takes something on our part to God-watch—our will—a willed choice to make it happen. With practice, our God-watching grows into a solid habit, and we find ourselves living with a conscious spiritual alertness that looks for God in all things, at all times. Ultimately with that alertness intact, again and again, we see Faithful Divine Provision showing up at our door.

Prayer suggestions

Pray to faithfully practice God-watching. Express to God how you desire to see the Divine move in your life. Ask to see God's provision for a need that you currently have. Thank God for the provisions you've received.

CHAPTER 14

Leaving Grief's Nest

"It is clear to me that I have not come to that knowledge; but one thing I do, letting go those things which are past, and stretching out to the things which are before, I go forward to the mark, even the reward of the high purpose of God in Christ Jesus."

(Philippians 3: 13-14 BBE)

A widow commented, "One of the hardest aspects of grief is giving it up."

Her telling words took me back to a springtime when birds built a nest on our front porch. Soon, it housed a clutch of gaping-mouthed fledglings. Mama bird dutifully fed until her brood until they learned to fly. Her job finished, her nest empty, she disappeared.

However, one of Mama's flock failed to understand the nesting process. Slow to grasp that the roost was not his permanent address, he returned to it daily. His tiny claws digging into its rim, he sat perched inspecting his vacated home, squawking loudly. His high-pitched cries seemed anxious inquiries. "Mama, are you here? Where did everyone go?"

I felt empathy for the dejected fledgling. Would he make it on his own? However, he had little choice. A new season of life had arrived, insisting he go it alone, take wing and discover a new existence, one richer than he could imagine or envision from the confines of his roost.

As a widow, I see simile in that bird's situation, a vivid illustration of what happens to widows after the loss of their spouse.

When we're first widowed, we immediately feel catapulted into a surreal and different environment, a nest of grief, so to speak. Naturally, we find this nest anything but cozy and comfortable. Its form is rough, needling us with sorrow. Its chaff unmercifully pricks, vexing us with unbearable heartache. Anguished, full of pain, we wish to flee from the horrid nest, but how can we fly laden with a grieving heart?

So—unless we foolishly, intentionally, fall out of grief's nest prematurely, thinking we don't need its home, or have time to spend in its confines—we find ourselves sitting captive in its roost heeding its demands for our undivided attention. Slowly we learn to yield, to let our pain help us to properly attend to grieving. In time, much to our surprise, the grieving we do seems to transform the nest. It evolves into a space where we feel secure, a private place allowing us to weep freely, a sanctuary of peaceful solitude where we heal and grow strong, equipping us to enter back into life's thoroughfare.

Unfortunately, our culture, stingy with giving the grieving adequate time to heal, calls us back to the line of duty oftentimes, far before we feel ready to exit the nest. Nonetheless, we rise. Grief's weighing on us heavily, we return to our jobs, to our family responsibilities—to all that is expected of us. Knowing protocol, we perform our duties well, present in body, but *without* heart and soul. They lay buried back in grief's roost, refusing to cooperate with life's demands or our society's unspoken rule to the grieving, *"Smile, pretend for our sake's that you're over your loss."*

At the end of each day, we sigh with relief. Crawling back into the comfort of the nest, thankful for reprieve, we sob. Grief assures us that here we don't have to pretend, we don't have to fight tears, or wear a faux smile.

However, a time will come when grief's roost, to every widow, starts to feel tight, shrunk in size. It's hard for us to see at that moment, that the intense grief that has been our "new-normal" for so long, now stabilized, no longer fits. It may take us a while before we recognize what many widows sense at this stage of widowhood. The blue feelings of discontentment, unsettledness, and wanting more purpose, indicate we've outgrown grief's nest. It's nature's call, her way of telling us, it's time to take wing—to leave the roost.

Explore and share

The writer of Philippians 3:13-14 (today's key verse) gives us the best flight path for our departure, a direct route to our objective. His finger on widowhood's map, he draws a line from grief's nest to our new beginning. His suggested route sounds simple but no widow finds it easy, "[Let] go of "those things which are past, and [stretch] out to the things which are before..."

For each of us, our nesting (grieving) time varies. When, finally, we start to feel ready to leave our nest-home, the complexity of leaving it dawns on us. Then, like the little bird on my front porch, uncertain of what's "out there," we may suddenly feel anxious, as if we're moving at too fast a pace. Familiar with the safety and the uncanny sense of security we've known in our personal nest of grief, it may seem preferable to remain glued to its roost, rather than cutting ourselves free from "those things which are past."

In today's exploration, we'll look for possible tethers that may be keeping us tied to our grief, to our past life. Then we'll look at God's plan to exchange our grief for joy, plus take a glance at what we can expect to encounter as we move fully into our new beginning.

Exercise 14:1

Any widow choosing to make of her widowhood a spiritual pilgrimage will probably, at some point, become aware of a tether or two. They are subtle little things, hard to recognize, small notions that keep us emotionally attached in some measure to our grieving and grief.

When a widow begins to feel a need for enlargement—to move beyond her grief—it's the perfect time for her to ask, *Am I presently, in any way, attached to my grief?*

Review the following statements voiced by widows, each of their remarks reveal a tether. Some are myths based on fear, others are indicative of the self-absorption that often comes with grieving. Explore the Scriptures given and the questions, keeping in mind the purpose of this exercise is to help us free ourselves to move forward. If in a group setting, share your thoughts.

Myth filled tethers:
I fear that, if I stop grieving my husband's loss, I will be betraying him, denying his memory—and then, if I'm not grieving his loss— I'm afraid my love for him could fade.

How does Song of Solomon 8:6a-b, speaking of the permanence of love, reveal that love—not grief—keeps one closely connected to the departed?

I don't want to let go of my grief because it's all I have left of my husband.

To a widow owning this statement as truth, how might heeding the call heard in Jeremiah 33:3 aid her in finding fresh vision for her life?

Tethers of self-absorption:
I know it sounds selfish, but I found my reason to hang on to some grief is because people are willing to do things for you when you're grieving. I don't know what I'd do without their help.

How might habitually using our widow status, knowingly or unknowingly, for selfish purposes, eventually permit grief and widowhood to define us—to box us into its role—hindering us from experiencing God's holy best?

I'm holding onto the past and grieving my loss as I've nothing else to live for. I'm an older widow, and too old to reinvent my life.

Ask yourself, do God's plans to give me the holy best really dry up with old age?

How might considering Jesus's reminder in Luke 17:32-33, help widows of all ages to see the often-sad result of holding on to the past?

Maybe your tether, if you discover one, is not on the list above. Write down what you believe may be holding you to your grief—to the past, and what you will do to untether yourself from it.

Exercise 14:2

Untethering ourselves is freeing, life-giving. It opens our hearts to reach out and fully possess the promises of God, especially regarding the promises made specifically to those who mourn. In exploring them, we'll view—the glorious hope of leaving our grief in the past—where it belongs.

Read Psalm 30:5b

- What is promised to those who weep?

Read Isaiah 61:3

To the mourning, God offers an exchange program. In this Scripture, what are the things God encourages us to trade, in exchange for what? Prayerfully, take a few minutes to view this verse as a personal contract you make with God, purposefully handing over to God the ashes of your loss, your mourning, and your despair to God. Consciously picture yourself receiving from the Divine Hand what this verse offers you in exchange for the vestiges of your grief.

Exercise 14:3

Untethered, we are in form to stretch out to the things which are before. Exactly what are we reaching for? What is it that lies before us? What does our future look like?

Philippians 3:14 answers these questions, telling us moving on will bring us to a "high purpose," a purpose greater than we can imagine. In the Scriptures below, let's explore the blessings that will literally "overtake" any who choose to wholeheartedly move forward, pursuing the Divine.

Read Deuteronomy 28:2-9

- What assurance, hope and comfort does this passage speak to your heart regarding you and your future?

Read Isaiah 43:1-2

- What promise do you find in this text, assuring you that God will remain at your side in every impossible situation you may face—presently—or in the future?

Read Romans 8:28

- How will pocketing this verse's truth into your heart, carrying it with you into your new beginning, allow you to experience peaceful assurance in "all" things?

***

As we've discovered thus far in our widowhood journey, when we choose to move forward, we will find ourselves going deeper into God's holy best. Choosing to cut ourselves free from tethers holding us to grief's nest is no exception; it is a gigantic step forward! Its action lifts us airborne, placing us on the best flight path to our new beginning, to a destiny rich in purpose and a future far richer than we could ever have imagined or envisioned from the rim of grief's nest.

Prayer suggestions

Pray for the Spirit to show you any tethers you are unaware of. Pray for courage and strength to leave the past and grief behind. Choose to purposefully believe God has good things planned for you and your future. Pray to fully believe in the mercy, grace and goodness of God that is always at work on your behalf.

CHAPTER 15

The One Thing Every Widow Needs

But few things are needed—or indeed only one. Mary has chosen what is better, and it will not be taken from her."

(Luke 10:42 NIV)

A t the handy man's request, I came outside to look at the new metal cellar doors he had just installed. I had specifically ordered the doors pre-primed and painted. However, in inspecting them, terribly disappointed and very upset, I complained to the man, "Look, the paint's scratched here and here," marking the spots with my finger.

He replied, as if he had no remembrance regarding the specifics of my order. "Oh, the doors are only primed. They don't come painted. You'll need to paint them yourself before winter."

My heart sunk, anger rose. My perfect plan to spare myself a painting job had miserably failed. If the man noticed tears of frustration welling in my eyes, he said nothing. I wanted to scream—to demand he return the doors—but with winter approaching, I needed them installed ASAP. I can't recall what all I said to the poor installer, but I do remember my attitude and actions definitely showed my darker side.

I didn't bother to consider that I might be overreacting, or that this really wasn't that big of a deal. To me, at that moment, a widow of two years, all I could think of was, *here I am again, overwhelmed with my widowhood, adding something else to my never-ending stress of trying to keep up with things.* I constantly felt like a juggler juggling umpteen dinner plates, trying to keep all of them in the air. Between my finances, the demands of a restoring a home needing much repair, being present for my children and grandchildren, and taking regular trips out-of-state to visit my aging parents, my juggling act had worn me down. Sorrowfully disappointed, I frequently would ponder, *so—this is how my new beginning looks?*

That day with the service man only accentuated my then-present disenchantment with life, and my disappointment in myself. Recently, I had noted growing outbursts similar to the one with the door installer. My rants mystified me.

Why was it that for periods of time, I would experience great peace and the joy of knowing the sweet, intimate fellowship of God's companionship, the wonderful sense of Christ living in and through me—but then—as soon as life threw too much at me, I would cave, losing the vividness of that union? Eventually, I found the answer. I came to understand that when anxiety arrests your attention, if allowed to remain and dominate your thoughts, it captures your heart, sadly diminishing your spiritual sense of God being with you.

A good illustration of anxiety and how it affects one's spiritual life is found in Luke 10:38-42. In this account, we find Jesus visiting the home shared by two sisters, Martha and Mary. The presence of Jesus, the renowned Teacher, attracted a number of guests to the sisters' house. As the story begins, we meet Martha, a plate-spinner like me, bustling about with nervous energy serving guests the food she had laboriously prepared for this event.

Martha's work of serving is her present priority, leaving no time for her to sit at Jesus' feet like her sister Mary is doing. As Martha buzzes about hosting, she reaches a point when her heart suddenly appears totally captured by anxiety. Its shrill is heard, loud and clear, in her tone as she addresses Jesus.

Martha's sibling, Mary, as the story shows, does not budge from her position at Jesus feet. Of course, her eyes, not blinded by anxiety, sees the event differently than her sister. Through eyes of love and adoration for Jesus, she views this as time for worship, not work—but then—worship seemed to be Mary's life's entire purpose and priority. It's obvious, Jesus remained her fixation. There was no room in her heart for anxiety; Jesus had captured her attention and her whole heart.

What is capturing your heart today? What is capturing my attention? Have you allowed anxiety to temporarily take your heart's throne, dismissing Jesus to take second place, as did Martha in today's story? That's a good question for all of us to ask ourselves as we explore ways to encourage our Mary-side to prevail.

Explore and share

To glean the most out of our exploration, let's put ourselves in the sisters' shoes, learning what we can from both, applying it to our own lives.

Exercise 15:1

Read Luke 10:38-42

Reviewing Martha's actions in this story can help us learn to better recognize indications of anxiety in our own lives. When we do discern its activity, below are questions we can ask ourselves to keep anxiety from capturing our hearts.

- In what way does stressed-out Martha show she's upset with Jesus? Ask yourself, *when I'm filled with anxiety, do I tend to inwardly point my blame finger at God, "Jesus, don't you care...?"* Am I willing to erase that thought when I hear it in my mind, choosing instead to see this as an occasion to exercise faith, voicing thanksgiving to God for the Divine's faithful care and love in all matters affecting me?

- What did Martha want Jesus to do to "fix" her present dilemma? When I live with anxiety, do I tell God what I want the Divine to do? Or, am I learning to still anxiety by praying, *"Jesus, what are you inviting me to learn, to see, to experience in this overwhelming situation?"*

- How does Jesus respond to Martha's fix-it idea? In what way does He suggest to Martha a "better" way than her frantic worry and frustration? *Am I willing to commit to praying, "God, please show me a better way than worrying and fretting, and I will practice what You reveal."*

Exercise 15:2

While Martha is seen in Luke's story as a whirlwind of anxious activity, Mary sits quietly, reverently at Jesus' feet, drinking in His every word. Some might explain the difference in the two sisters' priorities (Martha's busyness and Mary's quiet heart) as having to do with personality differences. However, that theory is debunked by Jesus's reproving words to Martha, subtly encouraging her to search for the "one thing" Mary had but she did not have.

Have you ever wondered, exactly what the "good part" is that Jesus said Mary had chosen, "that which would not be taken from her?" Our first inclination has us thinking it has to do with love. Let's explore that.

Read Matthew 22:37

Mary took seriously what Jesus called "The first and great commandment" (22:38). Her focus was on loving God fully—heart, soul, mind—every fiber of her being committed to—not just following Jesus, but—genuinely, wholeheartedly loving Him.

Ask yourself, *in what ways am I daily seeking to wholeheartedly deepen my love for God?*

Exercise 15:3

Anxiety is a real spiritual thwart when it comes to deepening our love for God. How so? It has a domino-like effect on us. First, anxiety in all its forms, takes our focus off of God, stealing our hope, keeping our eyes nervously glued to what is going on around us. Secondly, anxiety temporarily disables trust in God, and stalemates growing love for the Divine as we can only love someone to the degree that we trust them.

It stands to reason then, that one certain way in which we can cultivate growing love for God is by developing a quiet heart, a heart that lives watchfully, mindful of the first hint of anxiety's presence, instantly removing it before it sprouts full bloom, destroying hope.

Of course, our widowed lives, especially in living in today's chaotic world, will give us all too many happenstances with anxiety. It's important to consider these events not as a bane (although they are) but as the very thing we need in order to learn to maintain a quiet heart. In preparation for future visits from anxiety, let's explore the God-approved practices found in the following Scriptures. Employing these practices, will create and further develop within us a quiet heart that stays focused, trusting in God, ultimately transforming and enhancing our love-life with the Divine.

Read Exodus 14:13-14

- Moses, addressing the distraught Israelites who could see no hope in their situation, asks these people to do what, opening the way for them to see God do what? Does not God ask the same of us when we grow anxious?

Read Colossians 3:15a

- This verse asks that we permit what to rule in our hearts? How might that shield our minds from anxious thinking?

Read Psalm 37:7-8

- What key actions do these verses offer, vital to establishing a quiet heart?

Read Isaiah 30:15

- What does this verse promise to those who consistently return to the work of establishing and strengthening a quiet heart?

Read 1 Peter 3:4

- In God's eyes, what is the value of a quiet heart?

***

Living in a world that is falling apart, it often seems that chaos hides behind every corner, guaranteeing us, for as long as our feet stand planted on this planet, we *will* experience anxiety. However, that's not the issue. It's what we do with anxiety that matters. Do we let it stew within us, driving us, holding us captive, stealing hope from us? Or, do we let anxiety serve as a wakeup call, reminding us to immediately return to seeking a quiet heart—a heart dedicated to trusting and loving God fully?

Most definitely, anxiety places blinders on our spiritual eyes— but—when the heart lives in restful, quiet peace, the blinders fall off. Then we see truth crystal-clear again, we see, and feel the throbbing Presence of God alive within us—a Presence— which today's key verse assures, "cannot be taken from [us]."

What joy this truth brings to our Martha-side—why it's even sufficient to make a Mary of us! We are never without God's love or without God's company. No matter how we feel, no matter whatever chaotic mess is distracting us, even when our Martha-side is frantically spinning plates, God's sweet presence is with us, calling to us. *Stop. Cease fretting. Do not be afraid. Quit worrying. Be still...consciously breathe in...breath out, exhaling anxiety— until you sense quietness filling your soul—reawaking you to what is True—to the "One Thing" crucial for you to see yet again; I am here with you, just where you left Me when worry took over.*

It is precisely that One Thing—that One Holy Presence—that makes a widow's new beginning shine radiant with hope.

Prayer suggestions

Throughout your day, when you feel anxiety creeping in, reset your heart by praying Psalm 19:14. "Let the words of my mouth and the meditation of my heart be acceptable in Your sight, O Lord, my strength and Redeemer." Pray to take seriously the goal of obtaining and maintaining a quiet heart, creating space to trust and love God in greater measure.

Reaping Wholeness

"A time to weep and a time to laugh; A time to mourn, and a
time to dance."

Ecclesiastes 3: 4

CHAPTER 16

Living Whole

"The Lord proclaims, I remember your first love, your devotion
as a young bride, how you followed me..."
(Jeremiah 2:2 CEB)

L ife breaks everyone to some extent. However, if we listen, it teaches us how to heal and how to live whole. It's
a contradiction, isn't it? Life though, reveals many para-
doxes. From the devastated burnt forest floor comes new life.
A person's weaknesses often become that individual's greatest
strengths. Grief, as every widow discovers, although appearing
like an enemy initially, proves a comforting friend, healing our
brokenness, helping us to know wholeness.

Wholeness. Just what is that? Is it some mystical word without substance? If it's real, how does one know if and when they
are living in its zone?

Wholeness is difficult to define. We all experience it differently but basically, when we are living in its fullness, we know it
as an inner sense, a feeling of one's entire self—soul, mind, and
spirit—joined as one, at peace, flowing harmoniously together.
This harmony of self brings the soul into perfect alignment and

union with God, letting one experience the tremendous actuality of what Jesus Christ came to give abundant life (John 10:10).

Certainly, wholeness sounds like a wonderful state of being to live in continually, doesn't it? However, the human heart, no matter how spiritual it grows, maintains a tendency to get out of sync from time to time, losing that exquisite sense of wholeness. In those times, as pictured in today's Scripture, we revert to 'doing our own thing,' a "runaway bride," whose love has gone suddenly lukewarm.

In that same verse, we also catch a glimpse of God's love-hungry heart, sadly pleading for *our* return to harmony, to union with the Divine, to live again in wholeness. Perhaps we've never experienced living in the zone of wholeness—or we're as a bride on the run, but we can rest assured, God will keep on calling us home to wholeness. It's the nature of God to do so.

Explore and share

In today's exploration, let's probe for hindrances that might be prohibiting us from living in the zone of wholeness, and how we might overcome them.

Exercise 16:1

The following Scriptures ask us to consider what our heart is "wearing." Obviously, how our heart is clothed must be an important consideration for the one hungry to live in wholeness.

Read Ephesians 4:31

- What does this particular verse tell us to "put away"? What things are we to remove from our spiritual closets?

Read Colossians 3:12-14

- List the graces we are to "put on" so that we might be clothed in wholeness, enabling us to know delightful intimacy with God?

Exercise 16:2

In the previous exercise, the Colossians passage revealed graces for us to dress in, while the verse in Ephesians showed items *unsuitable* for our heart to wear. What if we feel unable to remove unbefitting garb from our heart, such as the anger that simmers inside us, the stingers of resentment that needle us, and bitterness that sours our perspective on just about everything?

Exploring the subject of forgiveness can help us undress our heart of the unsuitable, and redress it properly—clothing the heart with good—to include the grace with which we forgive others.

To begin our study, let's repeat a basic fact. Life breaks everyone to some extent. If those broken places are left untouched, our heart grows shrouded with anger, bitterness—maybe even hatred—creating turmoil within. How do we locate the incidents that have left us fragmented, so that we might mend, and find wholeness?

Many of the events that have left us marred reveal a "someone" that is negatively linked to the damage done to us. Therein, we discover a transgressor in need of our forgiveness. Maybe the injury inflicted came in childhood. Children, sensitive in nature, can be easily injured emotionally. Perhaps our childhood history includes abuse, acts of physical and sexual maltreatment that made victims of us, leaving us with a burden of shame and self-reproach, much too large for a child to bear. If we have yet to forgive our childhood transgressors, we still carry that burden today.

As adults, we've met plenty of transgressors, adding to our brokenness, placing extra names on our "need-to-forgive" list. Regretfully, transgressors are sometimes the people we love. For instance, marriage has broken many souls. When two people promise on their wedding day to love and cherish one another, but the union evolves into a battlefield, it turns the partners into transgressors. Then of course, abuse has been a part of some marriages. Whether the abuse was verbal, physical maltreatment, infidelity, or addictions, it stole one spouse's life, her/his dignity, and self-worth. Restoration is possible, but it does require forgiving the transgressing partner.

What if that one has passed? Whether our transgressors have died or still live, we must forgive them. To withhold forgiveness from them is to remain out of sync with God, leaving us in a state of un-wholeness—our hearts caustic, gnarled in anger. It's a miserable way to live life.

To the contrary, living in wholeness makes every moment of life worth living. The good news is, we head toward its zone every time we offer or ask forgiveness. The joy we find in giving forgiveness motivates us to make it a practice, doing regular spot checks, asking—*is there someone living or deceased, that transgressed me that I have yet to forgive—and whom have I trespassed against, for which I need to seek forgiveness?*

It's a question that will keep forgiveness up to date in our lives, allowing us to know harmony within, and a precious union with God.

Read Matthew 6: 9-13

- Reviewing the words that Christ taught us to pray, how optional is forgiving others?

Read Matthew 6:15

- If you choose not to forgive someone, what will be the outcome of that decision?

Read Psalm 130:3-4, 7-8

According to verse three:
- Who's without fault in this life? Who's in need of forgiveness for transgressions? Where is forgiveness found?

According to verses seven and eight:
- What is the extent of God's forgiveness and redemption, and how many of our sins is God willing to forgive?
- What kind of example do these verses set, giving us a pattern to follow in our personal work of forgiving our offenders?

Read Matthew 18:21-22

- How many times are we to forgive an individual?
- Could it be—we know when forgiveness is complete—when we begin to pray prayers seeking God's mercy and blessing to rest on our transgressor?

Exercise 16:3

In this particular exercise, let's consider times when, being perfectly honest with ourselves, we might say, "I know it's God's will for me to forgive, but I'm struggling. I'm not sure I can do it—or that I really want to forgive."

What then?

Perhaps such a struggle evolves as a result of us trying to forgive on our own. Apart from God, we have no personal, private stock of mercy from which to draw and forgive. The good news is that within us God's divine mercy flows like a mighty river. It is that mercy—God's own mercy—which we recycle, giving it out freely in holy acts of forgiveness, even when the one we forgive is, from a human standpoint, not deserving of mercy.

Read Psalm 108:4 and Psalm 103:17

Knowing it is God's mercy with which we forgive others, let's use the above verses to determine its holy boundaries. Seeing it measurements will help us to know the level of which we are to show others mercy.
- How boundless and fixed is God's merciful favor?
- How do these Scriptures help us to grasp some understanding of the deep level of mercy we are to offer to others?

Read Micah 7:18

- What does God delight in?
- Do my daily encounters with others reflect God's happy delight of showering humankind with the Divine's unmerited favor?

Proverbs 11:17

- If I strive to grow in mercy-giving, what will it do for my soul?

Matthew 5:7

- What do we receive in every act of mercy-giving?

Micah 6:8

- What does God require of us regarding mercy?

James 2:13

- What triumphs over judgement?
- How do our neighbors, family, and the strangers we meet, see us? As one who tends to judge, or as one who shows mercy?

***

When showing mercy and forgiving others, let's not overlook the need to show ourselves mercy, and to forgive ourselves. After all, God has forgiven us, so isn't it time to do the work of forgiving our self? Furthermore, we cannot personally know wholeness if we are withholding from ourselves forgiveness.

My widow friend Ruby came to such a point of understanding. Her widowhood story began when she returned home from work one particular day. She had a sense when she walked through the door and found the house silent that something was not right. She went upstairs and there she discovered her husband, dead. Severely depressed, doctors not having found effective medication for him, he had taken his life.

Ruby told me, "Knowing the anguish he had been suffering, I had no issue in forgiving him, but I couldn't forgive myself. Could I have done something to have spared him from taking his life? Was it something I did, or said that caused him to take that step?"

I asked her how and when she had come to finally forgive herself. Ruby seemed at a loss to my how-and-when question. She answered, "Well, I really don't know...,"

Ruby continued conversing, mentioning how she wore the blame for her spouse's death and the awful guilt that resulted from that, plus, carrying the great sorrow of losing the man she loved, his death untimely and cruel—all of it had left her devastated. Then I heard her say, "I found comfort in taking my husband's tattered old Bible that he loved and read faithfully to bed with me every night. I would hug it, holding it up against me. I did that for a year."

Those words triggered my spiritual imagination. I couldn't help but picture Ruby's husband somewhere in the great Beyond, asking God, "Please help my dear wife to know she's not to blame."

So, could it have been God at work, answering that prayer, by inspiring Ruby to retrieve her husband's beloved Bible? Night after night, as she slept, holding God's Holy Word up against her, mercy, self-forgiveness, and truth dripped drop by drop, into Ruby's heart, gradually setting her free, making her whole.

Her story brings my heart joy and assuring comfort. It tells me that mercy and forgiveness spoken by the human heart—enabled by God's grace living within it—holds sacred power; able to transcend life and death, space and logic, capable of traveling across divine airways, directly to the intended heart—living or deceased—proclaiming forgiving redemption.

Prayer suggestions

Pray to *delight God's heart* by showing others mercy and forgiveness. Forgiveness is a process; pray not to lose heart, to keep on forgiving until your heart is clear. When the Enemy of the Soul accuses you of not forgiving, and you know you have forgiven, turn the accusation into a prayer of praise, thanking God that Divine grace is keeping intact the forgiveness you've extended.

CHAPTER 17

Who Am I?

"If you forget about yourself and look to me, you'll find both yourself and me."

(Matthew 10:39b MSG)

I recall vividly the dreary day three weeks after John died when I stood by his grave weeping. Studying both his name and mine etched into the same tombstone, I struggled trying to ascertain exactly *who* was buried there. Was it only John—or was I there also? The question seemed reasonable— the old me, the woman who had called herself "John's wife" for thirty-six years—was silent. *Who am I,* I wondered, trying to label the personhood I was left with. She seemed a stranger walking about in my skin.

Of course, in those moments I was experiencing what all widows encounter in their loss—an identity crisis. The who-am-I-now inquiry is one of widowhood's biggest questions.

It's understandable considering that when our spouse lived, we owned an identity like most married couples have—a self-identity created by two—a mix, part wife-part husband—two hearts blended into one until death cruelly split the union. It leaves the surviving partner asking, "Who am I now?"

The issue is perplexing enough but what compounds it is that the widow usually hasn't a clue how to go about finding her true self. However, not only widows seem at a loss when it comes to finding their genuine self; everyone appears to have the same dilemma. I saw evidence of that at a training retreat I recently attended where part of the day's agenda centered on finding one's core identity.

The attendees were instructed to pair up as partners, taking turns. The listening partner was to ask the other, "Who are you," and then bless her cohort's response with the words, "God is merciful." This exercise continued until the responder ran out of things to say regarding her identity. Following the session, some retreaters, sharing how the exercise had worked for them, cited that their first response had been to describe their personhood as a parent, a spouse, or by stating their professional status; "I am a doctor...,"etc. However, they noted that with each subsequent asking, "Who are you?" it caused them to look deeper within, beyond the initial selfhood that shapes one's exterior self-image.

The retreat session confirmed that it's our human inclination to determine our self-identity (and often our worth) by the roles we play in life, by the things we accomplish, and/or by the talents we own. Once any of those things are lost to us, it can set off an identity crisis, which in the end, can help us to find a truer self than we've known prior.

Explore and share

Of course, since we are always growing and evolving as persons, as life moves on, even in non-crises moments, we can find ourselves rehearsing the 'who-am-I' question. What if, each time we found ourselves mulling over that inquiry, we would consider it God's voice, inviting us to probe much deeper than our external selfhood? It's a thought worthy of exploration considering the Psalmist's words, "Deep calls unto deep" (Psalm 42:7. His words form a beautiful picture of God's deepness calling to our deepest selfhood, making known its mystery to us, a *knowing* as Paul described in I Corinthians 13:12, to "know just as I also am known [by God]."

It makes absolute sense then, don't you think, that to get to know our truest self, all we have to do is to fall deeper into knowing our Creator? Some might say that plan sounds too vague, too simplistic, or too mystical of an approach to finding one's most genuine self, but today's Scripture verse supports this plan. Jesus said, "If you forget about yourself and look to me, you'll find both yourself and me" (Matthew 10:39b MSG).

My young, unmarried granddaughter, a true God-seeker, discovered that truth on her own. In a conversation with her, she spoke of her spiritual pilgrimage and her own journey to self-discovery. She said, "The more I find out who I am, the more I come to know God."

At the age of twenty-two, when she has all kinds of opportunities to dress her exterior self in various roles of life—and call that her identity—she has come to realize a spiritual reality that takes many of us a lifetime to discover. "It's in Christ that we find out who we are and what we are living for" (Ephesians 1:11a MSG).

The Christ route to knowing our self is God's idea. After all, it was Jesus, God's own DNA, who came to earth as The Light of the World, revealing to humankind the unfathomable nature of the Divine. Accordingly, in questing to know Christ and to grow Christ-like, our spirit life turns into a process of "becoming"—our self-identity growing ever and ever truer to the nature of our Creator—in Whose image we were created.

Exercise 17:1

Read Jeremiah 2:13

Life has many springs from which we drink in our attempts to quench the longing in our souls—that deep inner craving to own a selfhood—one that tells us we have worth. The problem is that the cisterns we dig to find satisfaction—a sense of worth—eventually leak, returning us to thirsting for something more.

- What "two evils" did these people commit and how are they related?
- What can we learn from this Scripture when it comes to our own personal searches for identity? Where should we begin our search?

Read John 4:9-15

In this passage, Christ meets a woman who has come to draw water from a well. Jesus, discerning the woman's emptiness, gently and graciously points out a telling fact about her life.

- What is the fact that indicates she had been looking in all the wrong places to find self-satisfaction and worth?
- What gift does Jesus offer to her, promising it as a Source that would satisfy her deepest soul-thirst for as long as she chose to draw from it?
- A widow's loss can definitely diminish her sense of personhood. How might this story of a broken woman finding wholeness, give us direction in our quest to answer "the who-am-I-now" question?

Read Hebrews 4:12

- What can help us discern our own heart, revealing places where we are seeking to dig wells of satisfaction, rather than drinking deeper of Christ's living water?

Exercise 17:2

In this exercise, consider the following Scriptures, all of which reveal methods, unlike cistern building, that promise us personal and spiritual growth, which are both essential to our becoming our truest self in God.

Hosea 6:3

- What does this verse prescribe we pursue? As beings created in God's image, how might seeking a deeper understanding of God enable us to discover and affirm our true identity?
- How much does continual, consistent prayer to know God factor into our pursuit for God-understanding?

Read Matthew 11:29

- What method of spiritual growth does Jesus recommend in this verse?
- What does Jesus say we will discover in being yoked to Him?
- How has being yoked to Christ enabled you to learn more about who you are/ who you are not? Ponder this. If in a group, share your experiences.

Read Joshua 1:8

- What does this verse call us to practice, and what outcome will result from diligently following that practice?

Exercise 17:3

Widows reading this chapter obviously want to own a selfhood that blesses them, versus one that defeats them. Regularly practicing the practices suggested in the previous exercise, insures a rewarding selfhood, full of blessing. However, those blessings can get blocked if, and when, we fall into the bad habit some of us practice of berating ourselves.

Rather than treating our personhood with the care, respect and kindness that we show to others, we often may treat ourselves in an opposite manner. Every time we personally do something we consider faulty, our behavior turncoats on us. We speak to our self with disgust, calling ourselves derogatory names, each one stealing pieces of our self-worth, each proclamation declaring us "stupid," or "incompetent, or... the list is endless. Additionally, our words regarding our physical appearance usually are equally as mean-spirited. Our berating self-talk, rehearsing in our head or spoken verbally is cruel punishment, enough to make our true self remain hidden, certain we'll ruthlessly criticize it as well, should it surface!

Let's review Scriptures that can help us kick the habit of self-berating, insuring our souls remain open to blessings.

Read John 8:36

Where is our liberation found, setting us free to become who we are divinely created to be?

Proverbs 23:23

- What does this verse say about any truth we purchase from God's Word?
- In what ways might we sell off our keen awareness of our value in God's sight? Might one of those ways be self-beratement?
- You and I know we are blessed people of God. In that case, could not our speaking disparaging things against ourselves personally offend our Creator?

***

One can hear relief, joy and freedom in Paul's voice as he states his identity, found in Christ. "I have been crucified in relation to the world, set free from the stifling atmosphere of pleasing others and fitting into the little patterns that they dictate" (Galatians 6:14b MSG).

This freedom comes to all of us when we take the Christ route to find our truest self. Immersing ourselves in pursing God, we are changed; transformed, allowing us to discover God in fuller measure, and better understand who we are. This discovery always surprises us confirming to us once more that each of us are unique individuals, divinely designed and crafted—earthen vessels formed in the image of God—containers holding Living Water, that which quenches our thirst for a selfhood of worth. It is a Well that will never run dry.

Prayer suggestions

Pray that your pursuit of God will remain fervent; the deeper you pursue God, the more you will know your true identity. Pray to be a friend to yourself, speaking to your personhood only what will build it up, not tear it down. Pray to have an open heart in allowing God to free you of your blind spots, from pseudo personas of identity. Thank God for creating beautiful you!

CHAPTER 18

Awakening Dreams— Discovering Purpose

"Enlighten me, lest I walk as one dead to life..."

Psalms for Praying (from Psalm 13)[1]

S ome of my fondest memories shared with John, my first husband, were the cozy chats we had down through the years--heartwarming conversations centered on our little family and the adventures we shared together. In later years, with our family nearly grown, our conversations shifted to dreams of what we would do as retirees. We held aspirations of paying off our home and financially helping our grandkids through college. Our biggest dream though was to sell our house, buy an RV and take off, spending our days in leisurely travel.

However, John passed away before those retirement years came, and with him went the dreams—dreams built for two. Facing retirement years alone, I wondered how I would find purpose. I had no dreams made for *just one*.

It's common for widows, their eyes glazed with grief, seeing their couple-sized, custom-built dreams vanished, to say, "I'm better off without dreams. Dreams will only disappoint you in the end."

Of course, those words come out of desolation. The widow's yesteryears had purpose, but now it seems, post-loss, that despondency's dark clouds shroud it, obscuring happy visions for the future. She can find herself echoing words spoken by grieving Job, "My days are past, my purposes are broken off..." (Job 17:11).

Unfortunately, oftentimes a lack of purpose seems to dog the widow, well past her grieving season, deep into the years of her widowhood. "I just go from day to day without any real sense of purpose," I've heard from widows' lips, mine included.

Purpose gives life meaning, and gives the soul life. It seems imperative then that we, as widows, should actively seek ways to infuse fresh purpose into our existence. This chapter concentrates on one particularly effective way to discover fresh purpose—the act of awakening and pursing our dreams.

Our dreams are a doorway to discovering our purpose. None of us are born without dreams. We come into life fully loaded, a stockpile of dreams within us—enough to last a lifetime. Creator God, the Maker of dreams, handpicked the specific ones you hold in your heart and the ones I hold in mine. Prior to our being fully formed in the womb, God—lovingly wove these dreams—like strands of colorful yarn, into the days fashioned for us (Psalm 139:16). The Divine now waits, longing for us to give breath to our God-instilled visions.

Like parents delighting to see their children unwrap presents picked for them, surely God gets great joy and pleasure in watching us unwrap our dreams, discovering in them pieces of our God-designed purpose, gifts that will permit us to make a positive difference in this world.

Explore and share

I believe the inspiration to write this chapter came to me eighteen years ago when I saw a table full of widows sitting at a church potluck dinner. Characteristic of such social gatherings, the room was abuzz with laughter and conversations between families gathered. However, at the widows' table, not a word flowed. Their faces spoke no emotion, but their eyes told plenty, revealing a tragic emptiness within them, the kind of hollow feeling inside the gut that tells a widow her life is over—her purpose is finished—there are no more dreams to be had.

The memory of those women still saddens me today, but unbeknownst to them, they taught me a lesson. A new widow at that time, I realized I could never afford to live without dreams to pursue—if I desired to know hope and purpose.

Exercise 18:1

Never is it as important to explore one's dreams as in the aftermath of a loss. At a time when life seems stripped of meaning, awakening our dreams injects into us fresh purpose. Let's consider the motivational power our dreams have.

Read I Corinthians 9:24

Our dreams call us to action, to engage in life, to know the energy of holy ambition.
- How does Paul, full of holy ambition, describe engagement with life?

Read Ephesians 3:20

God-breathed dreams hold divine empowerment—the power with which we birth our dreams.

- Through the lens of this verse, what might our dreams accomplish—what measure of purpose might they give to us?

Exercise 18:2

How do we start to awaken and unwrap our dreams? An *intentional*, purposeful exploration of them is the first step.

This exploration begins with excavating whatever dreams lie in our heart, to include digging up scraps of old dreams, stashed and perhaps deliberately "forgotten," also, unearthing present seed-dreams, visions we have not yet allowed to grow. Then the job of sorting and discerning begins, choosing which dreams may not be ours to embrace, and those that are awaiting us to give them breath. We do most of this excavation through prayer and reflection.

Read Matthew 7:7

- Regarding prayers for revelation of God-planted dreams within us, what does Jesus promise will result from *all* prayerful seeking?

Read Jeremiah 33:3

- Who is the Author of the great and mighty things written on our heart, of the things we are meant to pursue?

Prayer is the key to dream-exploration as it opens the heart and keeps it in listening mode, conditioned and ready to hear God speak. The Divine's voice is heard in a multitude of ways. We might discern a Divine-placed dream through: a movie we see, a sermon, or a song; through Scriptures, or other readings; through a conversation with a friend, or a passing chat with a stranger. Sometimes, revelation may come through a dream that occurs while we are sleeping. The point is, *intentionally* listening and watching for God's response to our prayers for discernment will yield revelation.

Prayers to recognize the dreams we're to embrace also helps us to discover and rout out self-designed dreams, those created by our ego-orientated-self; a selfhood that is expert at producing pompous visions, selfish in nature, such as to pursue wealth and fame. Then, of course, there are our self-driven dreams, the ones we cook up when we are starved for a taste of purpose; usually these "dreams" are a thrown-together mix, morsels of ideas that we hope will add some flavor and dimension to life.

Read Psalm 19:12-13

- How might praying this passage give us guidance in discerning ego-based, self-created dreams currently occupying our time and attention?

At this point, someone may ask, "How can I be a hundred-percent sure that my dream is God-based?" It's a good question, isn't it?

Read 2 Corinthians 5:7

Of course, no one can be absolutely certain of what they discern, but unless the holy guidance we hear is contrary to pursuing our dream, what does this verse reveal as the next step?

Exercise 18:3

What is it that we need to do to birth a dream? What is our part? What is God's part in that process? Throughout this exercise, write down your answers so you can review them for encouragement in any dream-building endeavor.

Read Mark 9:23

- What is essential in our seeking to birth a dream?

Read Hebrews 10:35-36

- What part does confidence and perseverance play in seeing the fruition of any dream?

Read Philippians 4:13

- In the often long and difficult process of dream birthing, from where will we draw the strength to endure, and the inspiration to carry our dream to the finish line?

Much of the difficulty we face in bringing our dreams to life lies within our person. For instance, fear can sabotage our dreams. Has fear caused you to think similar to the statements below?

- I've had a certain dream for years, but I don't have the qualifications or the understanding to pursue it. I wouldn't know where or how to start.
- If I was going to pursue my dream, I would have done it years ago; I'm too old now.
- I have mouths to feed, bills to pay, maybe another day I'll start to think about what my dreams are.

Only the truth can allay our fearful hesitancy. Consider then refuting your fears with these truths:

Read Psalm 32:8

- When we're uncertain how to proceed, what does God promise us?

Read Isaiah 41:10

- What provision does God promise to the less-than-bold dream builder?

Read 2 Corinthians 9:8

- As we step out in faith to pursue our dreams, how many of our needs will God provide for?
- How does this verse speak assurance to you regarding your God-planted dreams, that God will open the way for them to happen, regardless of what you lack , no matter your circumstances?

***

None of us have promise of tomorrow. This moment—today—remains the prime time to take courage and awaken our dreams, to let them soar; transporting us into the purposes God has uniquely planned for each of us.

Maybe the dream stirring in you is to write, to create music, or to express yourself through another art form. Maybe the dream growing in you will lead you to help the needy, or call you to social action, raising your voice for just causes—or perhaps—your dream will lead you to a new career path.

Then again, you may find your part in bringing a particular dream to life is simply to be a dream carrier, instilling the inspiration of dreams into another soul, such as King David did when he passed onto his son, Solomon, his dream blueprints for a magnificent temple he had wished to build for God. Like David, many parents are dream carriers, instilling in their offspring visions of making this world a better place.

Just think about it—every good thing ever done—began as a God-designed thought or dream within someone's heart. So, will you join me? Let's do some dream-seeking; asking God, "What dreams did You place in my heart long before my birth?"

In doing so, invariably, the God-dreams hidden within us will surface. As we unwrap them we'll find, in giving yesterday's dreams breath, life's greatest purpose being played out—to delight the heart of God.

That's when it dawns on the widow: in her heart lies a lifetime of God-dreams; dreams made—not for two— *just for one.*

Prayer suggestions

Ask God's Spirit to unveil God-placed dreams tucked within you. Pray for fresh faith, to believe God's anointing comes with every divinely inspired dream, enabling you to accomplish what is written on your heart to do. Pray for God's guidance, and to remain committed, full of enduring faith and strength to see your dream come to life.

CHAPTER 19

Dancing with Love

"You shall love the Lord your God with all your heart...You shall love your neighbor as yourself."

Mark 12:30a, 31a

Throughout William's eight-month war with terminal cancer, watching him decline, I often pondered how I would react to his death. I dreaded the void he would leave in my life. Ours had been an extraordinary marriage, a union of sweet companionship. We thrived in one another's company. In many ways, William's love for me seemed a mini simile of God's divine love in that William's presence gave me a sense of being "beloved," inviting me to live true to my authentic self. His actions always expressed, "I cherish you," even when I had acted less than my best.

No wonder I spent the last days of his life asking myself questions. How could I, in the absence of such marvelous love, hope to live whole? Would I respond to my loss of him as I had following John's death, running from grief and the emptiness of loss, caving into thoughtless whims? Would I ever love living life again? Only time would give me the answers.

Then, about a week prior to William's passing, I added another question—this one surfaced in a mini conversation he and I had one morning in our den where he laid on his hospital bed.

That particular morning, propped up with pillows, William sat with a fixed gaze, staring out the window at things I could neither see nor hear, his face shining. His eyes aglow with wonder, he repeatedly whispered revered awes of "Wow!"

Then, turning his head toward me, he said joyfully, "Okay, I'm ready. Let's go!"

Fighting tears, I said, "Oh Honey, I want to go with you, but I can't."

"Why not?" he responded obviously puzzled. In his clouded, medicated mind, there was no reason why I shouldn't accompany him. Hadn't we always traveled together?

My heart stood still, unsure of how to respond. Then, my mouth opened. It spoke without my permission, my voice flat. "I can't go with you William, because I have to finish my mission."

Unhappy with my answer, he said flippantly, "Okay, be that way." Obviously, to him my response registered as an excuse, probably because my words lacked conviction. I berated myself the rest of that day. *Why did I say what I did? I have no mission!*

Having experienced widowhood before, I had come to understand the difference between mission and purpose. I knew that the dreams God had instilled within me, such as writing, would allow me to know a sense of purpose again. However, the word mission seemed mysterious and daunting—something larger than purpose—like all-consuming work. Unable to shake free of the idea of it being an assignment, led me to ask, *Do I truly have a mission?*

I carried that question around for two years, as if in an open handbag, waiting for fate to rain down and fill it. Ironically, throughout that time, I remained ignorant of what was true—that I did have a mission—exactly as I had confessed to William. I was already on its path—a direct route, leading me out of bereavement into a dance with Love.

***

Explore and share

Regarding our mission in life Henri Nouwen writes, "We seldom realize fully that we are sent [into life] to fulfill God-given tasks. We act as if we have to choose how, where, and with whom to live. We act as if were simply dropped down in creation and have to decide how to entertain ourselves, until we die."[1]

Nouwen's words offer us a great sigh of relief, removing from us any notion that we have to find *our* mission. It's already been given to us. "Before I formed you in the womb I knew you; before you were born...I ordained you..." (Jeremiah 1:5).

What is it we have been God-ordained to do? What is our number one God-given task? Its assignment and job description are outlined in today's Scripture verse. "You shall love the Lord your God with all your heart...You shall love your neighbor as yourself."

Put in simple terms, our mission then, is a call to love: to live in the abundance of God's love, and to do on earth, the works of spreading that love.

This mission though, knows hindrances from the get-go. It's impossible for the human mind to fully comprehend the magnitude of God's love, so trying to convince our "neighbors" of its reality isn't simple. Sadly, sometimes we are the ones needing the convincing. Not understanding the fathomless boundaries of God's grace and mercy, we stumble, considering ourselves as unworthy and not "holy enough" to present ourselves before God to receive love. Consequently, we may sense the Divine in our lives only as The Great Judge, without any sense of knowing the

Divine as The Great Lover of our soul. Naturally, such shortsightedness keeps us abiding, not in God's love, but in fear.

However, hope takes heart, and faith gets a fair chance, as we seek to grow in the awareness of God's *real* Personhood, to view the genuineness of God. Accordingly, then, Who is this Divine One?

The first book of John answers, "For God is love" (4:8), written as if its author is determined to give us a mental picture of God. Taking his sketch tablet in hand, he puts on paper who God is and what God looks like. Holding the drawing up for all to see he says, "Look here, this is God"—can you see it now—"God is love."

As a child, the Scripture verse, 1 John 4:8, was a Sunday school memory-verse I learned. Growing up, I did not view its words as a picture portraying God, but as a demonstration of what God does; God loves people. That understanding wasn't flawed, just lacking. I had missed the key fact, as others have done. Looking closely at 1 John 4:8, we see that *love is* Who God *is*—God is the Holy Entity called Love.

Picturing God as Total Love—the dynamic Source from which all love flows—is to quickly sense God's magnetic love-force pulling, drawing us to the Divine (see John 6:44). So we discover in pursuing God that we actually are pursuing Love. It's a pursuit that makes of our following God not a religious duty, but a joyful encounter with Love, opening our eyes, maybe for the first time to see ourselves in God's mirror. In Song of Solomon 6:3 we see our image reflected: "I am my beloved's, and my beloved is mine."

It's a breathtaking, life-giving fact! You are—I am—God's beloved! Soak your feet in that truth for a moment. What difference will this marvelous fact make in your life—in mine?

When two people in love share their lives, their lives take on new meaning. There's a song in their hearts and a spring in their steps—and that's just human love! Multiply that scenario by mixing divine love with human love and you get a little bit of an idea how living in the Presence of Total Love might affect us.

Each of us will describe it differently, but all will agree; God's love mysteriously rejuvenates, energizes, and fills our soul with hope and gives to us a peace that surpasses all understanding. It is a love that literally fills us with bliss: an awesome knowing. We are cherished—adored by God.

I recall the years where, although I loved God, I did not know that kind of divine love relationship with God, nor did I view myself as God's beloved. I reflect on those years, seeing that long ago-self, much like a pauper given a great gift of a gorgeous mansion of many rooms, decorated with welcoming warmth, each room beautifully furnished, well stocked with every provision. In the kitchen, massive pantry shelves sat filled to the brim with food. Nevertheless, the pauper, as if sightless to the abundance that was now hers, chose to settle into but a tiny corner of one of the rooms. There she stayed. At night, she slept on a dirty blanket once retrieved from a trash bin. By day, she carefully divided the meager food she carried in her ratty backpack, hoping to stretch it out to make as many "meals' as possible—starving herself in the process.

I was that pauper spiritually. Maybe you feel the same way. Somewhere in our religious history, we bought an erroneous truth that many own. "You can have only 'this much and no more' of God's love this side of heaven." Living life with that belief leaves us half-starved spiritually, dearly wishing that God had made it possible for us to experience Divine Love in such a manner that we could experience degrees of heaven on earth.

The glory is that God did make that possible! It took an act of the Holy Trinity to bring it about The Spirit of Divine Love, giving all and sending Love Incarnate into the world, His life paid the price to dress us in robes of righteousness. Dressed in this glory, our spiritual beauty shining like the noonday sun, we are fully outfitted to successfully complete our mission of love.

God, fully pleased, like a stunned lover says, "[You are] perfect through My splendor which I [have] bestowed on you" (Ezekiel 16:14). It's a beautiful sight—us beholding God, God beholding us—the Divine and the human lost in the wonder of Total Love. Indeed, it is a relationship that brings a glorious touch of heaven to our earthly life.

Interestingly, something amazing happens in our pursuit of Divine Love. It enlarges our heart toward others. Our vision also changes. Through the lens of Total Love, remembering afresh that Christ gave His all for *all* peoples, we begin to *see* our neighbors—the people we have had a hard time tolerating, the folk who have different ideas and values than ours, those we may have snubbed for their poor behavior—as God's beloved.

"God doesn't love us only for us to feel beloved, but to give that love away," I've heard my pastor say. Interestingly, we clearly see then that pursuing Love leads us to fulfil the other half of our mission: to recognize our neighbors as God's beloved and to love them as such.

Love is given out in many varied ways. Maybe we give our time and money providing for the less fortunate. Generously lavishing God's love on others may have us volunteering as a tutor, working with an organization such as Hospice, sitting with the widowed, or with persons nearing their final hour of life. Sometimes offering Total Love is a challenge, like in speaking grace and forgiveness to someone who has not treated us fairly.

The beautiful thing is, no longer shortsighted and in love with the One called Love, giving away life's greatest gift—God's love—becomes our obsession, a mission we cherish. It's an all-consuming work we do hand-in-hand with our Beloved.

Today's Exercise

- Has this chapter spoken to you? In what ways?

Having a general awareness of a truth is only a beginning. To make it entirely ours, we have to personally embrace it. For instance, you are God's beloved:

- Where are you in your journey of growing into that knowledge?
- So far, how do you see the understanding of your belovedness reflected in your personal life?
- How has walking in the light of this awareness changed you?
- How does the knowledge of your belovedness provide insight as to how "to love your neighbor as yourself," as Christ commanded?

***

In discovering and embracing the mission God has given all of us, and claiming our belovedness, we find, at last, our mourning has evolved into dancing (Psalm 30:11); a beautiful dance with Love, our Beloved.

Living in union with Love, our mission is our passion, which keeps us focused on seeking ways to wildly, lavishly give Love's abundance away—each giving cost us something of our self, but in that we find in reward. It returns to us the taste of something that has been missing for a long time—the scrumptious sweetness of being fully alive, and loving life!

Prayer suggestions

Thank God that you are the Divine's beloved; pray to live in the ecstasy of that reality. Pray for a God hunger to continually fall deeper in love with God. Pray to see all those you encounter each day as God's beloved. Pray for courage to reach out in love to others.

An Endless Journey: Traveling in Love from Glory to Glory

"Though now you do not see Him, yet believing, you rejoice
with joy inexpressible and full of glory."
1 Peter 1:8

Glancing momentarily back to the beginning of our widowhood, some of us no doubt, as I did, considered it a bane. At that point, those like me wondered, "Is there any promise at all in this thing called widowhood?"

We remember those gloom-filled days well. Days when hope seemed a constant struggle to attain and to keep alive, when widowhood seemed to claim our identity, our strength and our joy, when grief held us captive night and day, when the question lived within us, *how will I ever survive widowhood?*

Yet, here we are—survivors, each of us with a story to tell. For many, like me, we came to a desperate point of recognition, realizing that our only hope to survive widowhood was to make of it a spiritual pilgrimage. In setting out on it we began to discover that widowhood *does* hold promise of blessings in abundant measure. As we traveled the various routes marked on widowhood's map, the Scriptures as our guidebook, we sensed a progressive transformation happening in us, evidenced by the return of hope to our lives.

Today we realize that our widowed life could have told a very sad story, an account verifying that widowhood had left us without purpose, with years full of empty days. However, thank God, true spiritual pilgrimages never end that way. They tell stories like our own, accounts of inevitable blessings, of hope ever-growing within, of eyes opening to the reality of God's Holy Presence, forever in us, and with us. They tell of hearing God daily whispering to our heart, "You are my beloved."

Our story, of course, is still being written. It's an account that will continue to tell of witnessing God's glory on earth, of sharing God's love with others. It's a story we can share with other widows, giving them hope, telling them of a joyful, hope filled pilgrimage, an eternal journey of traveling hand in hand with Divine Love, going from "glory to glory" (2 Corinthians 3:18).

Notes

Introduction
1. Johnston, William, ed. The Cloud of Unknowing. New York: Doubleday, 1973, p 141.

Chapter One. Longing for a Taste of Hope
1. Beattie, Melody. Journey to the Heart: Daily Mediations on the Path to Freeing Your Soul. San Francisco: Harper San Francisco, 1996, p. 174.
2. Nouwen, Henri. *Out of Solitude.* Notre Dame, IN: Ava Maria Press, 2005, p. 57.

Chapter Two. Finding Hope in a Muddle of Mistakes
1. Chittister, Joan. *The Breath of the Soul: Reflections on Prayer.* New London, CT: Twenty-Third Publications, 2009, p. 60. Used by permission.
2. Chittister, Joan. *God's Tender Mercy.* New London, CT: Twenty-third Publications, 2010, p. 34. Used by permission.

Chapter Three. Doing the Task of Grieving: Releasing Hope
1. Bennett, Paul. *Loving Grief.* Burdett, NY: Larson Publications, 2009, p. 74.

Chapter Four. Seeking Hope When Faith Lies Shattered
1. Gomes, Peter. *The Good Book.* NY: Avon Books, 1996.
2. Lewis, C.S. *A Grief Observed.* NY: Harper/Collins, 1994, p.66.

Chapter Five. Hope: Out of Season

1. Dillard, Annie. Three By Annie Dillard. NY: HarperCollins Publishers, 1990, p. 256.

Chapter Six. Taking Flight on Wings of Hope
1. Dickinson, Emily. "Hope is the thing with feathers." (1891).
2.. Carmichael, Amy. *His Thoughts Said...His Father Said...* © 1941 The Dohnavur Fellowship. Used by permission of CLC Publications. May not be further reproduced. All rights reserved.

Chapter Eleven. When There's No End in Sight—Cling!
1.   http://www.goodreads.com/author/quotes/11842543.Eugene_Peterson. Accessed May 17, 2017.

Chapter Eighteen. Awakening Dreams—Discovering Purpose
1. Merrill, Nan C. *Psalms for Praying: An Invitation to Wholeness.* London: Bloomsbury Publishing, 2007, p. 17.

Chapter Nineteen. Dancing with Love
1. Nouwen, Henri. *Bread for the Journey: A Daybook of Wisdom and Faith.* NY: Harper San Francisco, 1997, April 23rd reading.